W9-CHI-618

DISCOVERING CAREERS

Math

Titles in the
Discovering Careers
series

Adventure
Animals
Computers
Construction
Environment
Health
Math
Nature
Science
Space Exploration
Sports
Transportation

DISCOVERING CAREERS

Math

Ferguson's

An Infobase Learning Company

Discovering Careers: Math

Ferguson's
An imprint of Infobase Learning
132 West 31st Street
New York NY 10001

Library of Congress Cataloging-in-Publication Data

Math.
    p. cm. — (Discovering careers)
Includes bibliographical references and index.
ISBN-13: 978-0-8160-8052-6 (hardcover : alk. paper)
ISBN-10: 0-8160-8052-6 (hardcover : alk. paper) 1. Mathematics—Vocational guidance—Juvenile literature. 2. Mathematics teachers—Vocational guidance—Juvenile literature. I. Ferguson Publishing.
QA10.5.M387 2011   510.23—dc22
2010040590

Ferguson's books are available at special discounts when purchased in bulk quantities for businesses, associations, institutions, or sales promotions. Please call our Special Sales Department in New York at (212) 967-8800 or (800) 322-8755.

You can find Ferguson's on the World Wide Web at http://www.fergpubco.com

Text design by Erik Lindstrom and Erika K. Arroyo
Composition by Erika K. Arroyo
Cover printed by Bang Printing, Brainerd, MN
Book printed and bound by Bang Printing, Brainerd, MN
Date printed: March 2011

Printed in the United States of America

10 9 8 7 6 5 4 3 2 1

This book is printed on acid-free paper.

CONTENTS

Introduction

You may not have decided yet what you want to be in the future. And you don't have to decide right away. You do know that right now you are interested in mathematics. Do any of the statements below describe you? If so, you may want to begin thinking about what a career in math might mean for you.

_____ Math is my favorite subject in school.
_____ I like to work on math problems.
_____ I enjoy using computers.
_____ I like number games.
_____ I like strategy games, such as chess.
_____ I am interested in astronomy.
_____ I like to keep statistics for sports teams and other activities.
_____ I keep careful track of my money.
_____ I am curious about how things work.
_____ I am good at observing small details.
_____ I like to solve problems.
_____ I like science.
_____ I like to take things apart and see if I can put them back together.
_____ I like to invent things.

Discovering Careers: Math is a book about careers in math, from Accountants to Statisticians. Math is important in dozens of careers in government, science, business, and industry. Computers, banking and finance, physics, and engineering are all based on mathematics.

This book describes many possibilities for future careers in math. Read through it and see how different math careers are connected. For example, if you are interested in money and banking, you will want to read the chapters on Accountants and Auditors, Actuaries, Bank Services Workers, Bookkeepers, and Financial Planners. If you are interested in computers, you will want to read the chapters on Computer Systems Analysts, Software Designers, and Software Engineers. If you are interested in applying your interest in math to careers in engineering, you will want to check out the chapter on Engineers and Engineering Technicians. Or if you are interested in space careers, you will want to check out the articles on Astronomers and Physicists. Go ahead and explore!

What Do Math Specialists Do?

The first section of each chapter begins with a heading such as "What Demographers Do" or "What Statisticians Do." It tells what it's like to work at a particular job. It describes typical responsibilities and assignments. You will find out about working conditions. Do they work in offices or laboratories? Do they use computers? What other tools and equipment do they use? This section answers all these questions.

How Do I Become a Math Specialist?

The section called "Education and Training" tells you what schooling you need for employment in each job—a high school diploma, training at a junior college, a college degree, or more. It also talks about on-the-job training that you could expect to receive after you're hired.

How Much Do Math Specialists Earn?

The "Earnings" section gives the average salary figures for the job described in the chapter. These figures provide you with a general idea of how much money people with this job can make.

Keep in mind that many people really earn more or less than the amounts given here because actual salaries depend on many different things, such as the size of the company, the location of the company, and the amount of education, training, and experience you have. Generally, but not always, bigger companies located in major cities pay more than smaller ones in smaller cities and towns, and people with more education, training, and experience earn more. Also remember that these figures are current averages. They will probably be different by the time you are ready to enter the workforce.

What Will the Future Be Like for Math Specialists?

The "Outlook" section discusses the employment outlook for the career: whether the total number of people employed in this career will increase or decrease in the coming years and whether jobs in this field will be easy or hard to find. These predictions are based on economic conditions, the size and makeup of the population, foreign competition, and new technology. They come from the U.S. Department of Labor, professional associations, and other sources.

Keep in mind that these predictions are general statements. No one knows for sure what the future will be like. Also remember that the employment outlook is a general statement about an industry and does not necessarily apply to everyone. A determined and talented person may be able to find a job in an industry or career with the worst outlook. And a person without ambition and without proper training will find it difficult to find a job in even a booming industry or career field.

Where Can I Find More Information?

Each chapter includes a sidebar called "For More Info." It lists resources that you can contact to find out more about the field and careers in the field. You will find names, addresses, phone numbers, email addresses, and Web sites of math-related associations and organizations.

Extras

Every chapter has a few extras. There are photos that show math workers in action. There are sidebars and notes on ways to explore the field, lists of recommended personal and professional qualities, fun facts, profiles of people in the field, and lists of Web sites and books that might be helpful.

At the end of the book you will find three additional sections: "Glossary," "Browse and Learn More," and "Index." The Glossary gives brief definitions of words that relate to education, career training, or employment that you may be unfamiliar with. The Browse and Learn More section lists math-related books, periodicals, and Web sites to explore. The Index includes all the job titles mentioned in the book.

It's not too soon to think about your future. We hope you discover several possible career choices. Happy hunting!

Accountants and Auditors

What Accountants and Auditors Do

Accountants and auditors have long been called "bean counters." Their work has been considered boring and tedious. People used to associate them with death, taxes, and bad news. But that has changed. Accountants and auditors do much more than record financial information. Computers now count the "beans" while accountants and auditors analyze the results.

Accountants are numbers people. They are in charge of all of the financial records of an individual, business, or other organization. For example, accountants hired by a company add and subtract how much the company makes and spends over a given period of a time, such as a month. They calculate how much money is spent on operating costs. Examples of operating costs are bills for electricity, rent, and the use and repair of office equipment, such as computers. Accountants also measure a company's revenue, which is how much money comes in through the sales of products or services.

An accountant for a bakery, for example, looks at how much was spent to pay the workers, how much was spent to operate the bakery ovens, and how much was spent to buy the ingredients to make the bread and other products. These costs are called debits and are subtracted from the company's bank account. Then the accountant would calculate the money coming in from the sales of bread, cookies, cakes, and other goods the bakery sells. After the books (financial records) are closed for each accounting period (such as a month), the accountant prepares reports

EXPLORING

- Learn more about this career by checking out books at your local library and exploring accounting/auditing association Web sites. Here is one Web site suggestion: Start Here, Go Places (http://www.startheregoplaces.com).
- Keeping the financial records of a school club is an excellent way to explore the work of accountants.
- Get a job in a retail business, either part time or during the summer. Working at the cash register or even pricing products as a stockperson is good introductory experience.
- Talk to an accounting professional about his or her career. Ask the following questions: What made you want to enter the field? What do you like most and least about your job? How did you train for this career? What advice would you give to someone interested in the career? What is the employment outlook?

that will show whether or not a profit was made for that time period. These reports are then given to the president or owner of the company so he or she can make decisions about how to operate business during the immediate and long-term future.

Accountants not only review financial records, they also set up systems to keep track of the way money is handled. For example, if a company does not record expenses and income on a daily basis, an accountant might create such a bookkeeping system. Accountants often use computers to help keep track of financial records and solve mathematical problems.

Auditors are specialized accountants who study the business and financial records of a company. They do this to make sure the records are correct and complete. They help the company prevent mistakes and follow the laws for company record keeping. After they examine the records, auditors give reports to the company's managers and suggest ways to improve their record-keeping practices.

There are several kinds of auditors. *Internal auditors* are employees of a company. They help the company's accountants keep accurate records. They may also examine records to make sure employees are not using the company's money and property improperly. *Independent auditors* work for a separate auditing company. Businesses hire them on a temporary basis to check their records and to make sure their own auditors and accountants are accurate. *Tax auditors* examine taxpayers' records to figure the correct amount of taxes they owe. Most tax auditors work for the state or federal government.

Tips for Success

To be a successful accountant or auditor, you should

- love mathematics and working with numbers
- have strong mathematical, analytical, and problem-solving skills
- be able to think logically and to interpret facts and figures accurately
- have excellent communication skills
- be very attentive to detail

Accountants and auditors work for private companies and government agencies. About 24 percent work for accounting, tax preparation, bookkeeping, and payroll services firms. Only about 8 percent are self-employed.

Education and Training

If you are considering a career as an accountant or auditor, you should be good at mathematics and enjoy working with numbers. In high school, take classes in math and English, as well as bookkeeping and other business courses.

A college education with a major in accounting is the best way to prepare to be an accountant or auditor. Private business schools, junior colleges, and some technical schools also offer training programs. In these programs, students take courses in math, statistics, accounting methods, and computer science.

DID YOU KNOW?

- Accounting records and bookkeeping methods have been used since ancient times. Records discovered in Babylonia (modern-day Iraq) date back to 3600 B.C. Accounts were also kept by the ancient Greeks and the Romans.
- Modern accounting began with double-entry bookkeeping, which was developed by Luca Pacioli (c.1450–c.1520), an Italian mathematician.
- The accounting profession in the United States dates back only to 1880, when English and Scottish investors began to buy stock (a representation of financial ownership) in American companies. To keep an eye on their investments, they sent over accountants. When the accountants saw the great opportunities in the accounting field, they stayed in America to establish their own businesses. The U.S. government started to collect income tax in 1913.

Although any type of training in accounting is valuable, people with a college degree will usually find higher paying jobs. Many accountants also pass a state examination and obtain a license to practice as certified public accountants.

Earnings

New graduates with a bachelor's degree in accounting received average starting offers of $48,993 in 2009, according to the National Association of Colleges and Employers. Those with master's degrees in accounting were offered $49,786.

Salaries for accountants and auditors vary according to their experience, the type of business that employs them, and the difficulty of the accounting systems they work with. Accountants and auditors earned an average salary of $59,430 in 2008, according to the U.S. Department of Labor. The most experienced accountants and auditors earned more than $102,000. Accountants and auditors who work for the federal government earn more than those in private industry.

FOR MORE INFO

For industry information, contact
American Institute of Certified Public Accountants
1211 Avenue of the Americas
New York, NY 10036-8775
212-596-6200
http://www.aicpa.org

For information on women in accounting, contact
The Educational Foundation for Women in Accounting
136 South Keowee Street
Dayton, OH 45402-2241
937-424-3391
info@efwa.org
http://www.efwa.org

For information on internal auditing and certification, contact
Institute of Internal Auditors
247 Maitland Avenue
Altamonte Springs, FL 32701-4201
407-937-1100
iia@theiia.org
http://www.theiia.org

For information about management accounting and certification, contact
Institute of Management Accountants
10 Paragon Drive
Montvale, NJ 07645-1718
800-638-4427
ima@imanet.org
http://www.imanet.org

Outlook

The job outlook for skilled accountants and auditors through the next decade is excellent. More and more professionals will be needed to check the financial records of businesses, government agencies, and other organizations. Some accountants and auditors will work for banks and large companies, and others will work on their own. Many accountants, especially certified public accountants, will help people with their tax returns.

Actuaries

What Actuaries Do

Actuaries are mathematicians who design and plan insurance and pension programs for businesses. An insurance program usually covers the health or life insurance that a company offers its employees. Pension is money paid to a worker after retirement. Actuaries make mathematical calculations to help insurance companies figure out how much money they may have to pay to the businesses and workers they insure. They also figure out how much the policies should cost.

Insurance policies are formal agreements between insurance companies and policyholders. The policyholder pays a certain amount of money for the policy. This is usually a monthly fee called a premium. In return, the insurance company agrees to pay money to policyholders if they later suffer certain financial losses, such as those caused by accidents, illness, unemployment, or death. For example, if an insurance policyholder has a car accident, he or she files a claim with the insurance company. The claim shows the cost of the accident, including the cost to repair damage to the car or the amount of doctor bills to treat injuries. Insurance companies have created many different kinds of insurance, including life, medical, automobile, fire, and unemployment insurance. Many insurance companies also may handle pension programs.

Actuaries try to predict the number of policyholders who will have losses and how much money the insurance company will have to pay in claims. They then help the insurance com-

EXPLORING

- Visit Be an Actuary (http://www.beanactuary.org) to learn more about the career, read a list of suggested high school classes and personal skills, and view videos about the field.
- If you are interested in becoming an actuary, try activities that allow you to practice strategy and problem-solving skills. For example, you might join the school chess club, math club, or investment club.
- Participate in other activities that teach you leadership and management, such as student council positions.
- Visit the Web sites of colleges and universities that offer actuarial science programs to learn more about typical classes and educational requirements.
- Talk to an actuary about his or her career.

pany set prices for policies so that it always will have enough money to pay all the claims.

Actuaries use their knowledge of mathematics, probability, statistics, and principles of finance and business. Usually they begin by collecting and studying facts about events such as births, deaths, marriage, and employment. They then make tables to show the rates at which deaths, accidents, sickness, disability (when a person is injured or too sick to work), or retirement occur. For example, when they set the cost for earthquake insurance, actuaries look at how often an earthquake happens in the homeowner's area. If the owner lives in California, the insurance is going to cost more than for someone who lives in Kansas, because California has so many more earthquakes than Kansas does. But the tornado insurance for a Kansas home will cost more than for a home in California, because Kansas has a lot of tornadoes and California does not.

DID YOU KNOW?

- The term *actuary* was used for the first time in 1762 in the charter for the Equitable Society of London, the first life insurance company to use scientific data in figuring premiums. The basis of actuarial work started when French mathematicians Blaise Pascal (1623–62) and Pierre de Fermat (1601–65) figured out a way to calculate actuarial probabilities. Their work resulted in what is now called the science of probability.
- The first mortality table was produced when Edmund Halley (1656–1742) noticed that there were more male births than female births, and noticed that other such life events happened at regular intervals. Halley, the English astronomer for whom Halley's Comet is named, is known as the father of life insurance.
- In 1889, a small group of actuaries formed the Actuarial Society of America. Two classes of members, fellows and associates, were created seven years later, and special examinations were developed to determine membership eligibility. Forms of these examinations are still used today. By 1909 the American Institute of Actuaries was created, and in 1949 these two groups joined into the present Society of Actuaries.

To be a successful actuary, you should have good problem-solving skills, a curious personality, and be able to concentrate for long periods of time on detailed work. You also need strong communication skills in order to explain and interpret complex work to your clients. Other key skills for actuaries are ambition, motivation, and strong ethics (the code of rules about how we should treat others).

Education and Training

To be an actuary, you must like math and be able to do careful, detailed work. In high school you should take as many math courses (especially calculus and statistics) as possible. Computer science (especially programming) is also important. After high school you will have to go to college to earn a bachelor's degree in mathematics, statistics, economics, or finance.

Employers prefer to hire actuaries who have successfully passed a series of special examinations. The first two of these examinations should be taken while still in college. Actuaries usually take the other exams after they start working.

Earnings

Starting salaries for actuaries with bachelor's degrees in actuarial science averaged $56,320 in 2009, according to the National Association of Colleges and Employers. New college graduates who have not passed any actuarial examinations earn slightly less. Insurance companies and consulting firms offer merit pay increases or bonuses to those who pass examinations.

The U.S. Department of Labor reports that actuaries earned a median annual salary of $84,810 in 2008. Salaries ranged from less than $49,000 to more than $160,000.

Outlook

Strong competition is expected for actuaries during the next decade. The entrance requirements are very demanding, which causes many people to pursue careers in other fields. Opportunities should be best for actuaries who work for consulting firms.

DID YOU KNOW?

Where Actuaries Work

These are the most common places where actuaries work:

- Insurance industry—property (home) and casualty (car)
- Life and annuities
- Employee benefits
- Pensions
- Health
- Social Security
- Financial industry
- Banks, investing, risk management

Other places where actuaries work are:

- Consulting firms
- Government insurance departments
- Colleges and universities
- Large corporations
- Public accounting firms

Source: Casualty Actuarial Society

FOR MORE INFO

For general information about actuary careers, contact

American Academy of Actuaries
1850 M Street, NW, Suite 300
Washington, DC 20036-5805
202-223-8196
http://www.actuary.org

For information on careers in mathematics, contact

American Mathematical Society
201 Charles Street
Providence, RI 02904-2213
800-321-4AMS
ams@ams.org
http://www.ams.org

For information on the career of actuary, contact

Casualty Actuarial Society
4350 North Fairfax Drive, Suite 250
Arlington, VA 22203-1620
703-276-3100
office@casact.org
http://www.casact.org

For industry information, contact

Society of Actuaries
475 North Martingale Road, Suite 600
Schaumburg, IL 60173-2265
847-706-3500
http://www.soa.org

Architects

What Architects Do

Architects create plans and designs for buildings and sometimes the land surrounding the buildings. Shopping malls, schools, airports, offices, factories, and homes all began as designs on an architect's drawing table or computer screen. Many architects focus on one kind of building. Some design homes and office buildings. Others design sports arenas, theaters, churches or other religious structures, or manufacturing plants. They may also specialize in interior design or renovations (rebuilding) of existing buildings.

Architects begin an assignment by talking with their clients. The clients tell the architect how much money they can afford to spend, what type of building they want designed, and the date they would like the building completed. Then the architect makes some rough drawings. Eventually, blueprints are prepared that show the exact measurements of every part of the building or area. There will be floor blueprints, wiring blueprints, piping blueprints, and blueprints for the interior and exterior walls. The architect usually creates a realistic drawing of the interior and exterior to show the client what the finished product will look like. For large projects or public buildings, the architect may even create a small model of the building or produce one using a computer design program. Once construction begins, architects visit the work site. They answer questions and make sure the builders are following the plans.

EXPLORING

- Reading books and magazines about architecture will give you a good understanding of the nature of the work.
- Visit architecture-related Web sites. Here are some interesting Web sites to visit: ARCHcareers.org (http://www.archcareers.org), ARCHCareers Blog (http://archcareers.blogspot.com), and Great-Buildings (http://www.great-buildings.com).
- Most architects will welcome the opportunity to talk with you about the field. You may be able to visit their offices to see firsthand the type of work done by architects.
- Practice designing and building small structures, such as dollhouses, tree houses, and birdhouses.
- You can also build models of larger structures. Your local art and craft store may have model building supplies, such as scaled-down furniture, trees and shrubs, flooring, and siding.
- Take architectural tours in your city and anywhere you vacation.
- Ask your teacher or counselor to help set up an informational interview with an architect.

Architects must be familiar with zoning laws and local and state building regulations, including plumbing, electrical, heating, and ventilation (air flow) codes. They have to know construction methods and engineering principles. They must also consider the area's climate (temperature and other typical weather conditions), soil type (different soil types require different building methods and materials), and other environmental conditions. They also use architectural history to see how other architects have solved building design problems in the past.

Two architects review blueprints at a job site. (PhotoDisc)

Education and Training

To prepare for a career as an architect you should take shop classes (especially courses in drafting), computer-aided design, math, and art (especially free-hand drawing) in high school. History, English, writing, and art history are also important.

To become an architect you must complete a degree program at an architectural school. Most schools of architecture offer degrees through either a five-year bachelor's program, a three- or four-year master's program, or a two-year master of architecture program for students who have earned a preprofessional undergraduate degree in architecture or a related area. Most architecture students seek out the bachelor's degree in architecture. They go from high school directly into a five-year program.

Profile: Mies van der Rohe (1886–1969)

Mies van der Rohe was one of the leaders of the International style of architecture. He was known for his elegant but plain steel-and-glass buildings. Classic simplicity and precise proportions mark such works as Crown Hall at Illinois Institute of Technology (1955), the Dirksen Building, part of the Federal Center in Chicago (1964), and the National Gallery in Berlin (1968).

Mies van der Rohe's buildings at 860 Lake Shore Drive in Chicago, a striking innovation when built in 1951, helped establish the steel skeleton, glass-wall structure as a major building type. His technically efficient, sophisticated style, sometimes called "Miesian," was adapted by architects throughout the Western world.

Other buildings designed by the German-born American architect include Farnsworth House in Plano, Illinois; the Seagram Building in New York City, designed with Philip Johnson (another well-known architect); the Houston Museum of Fine Arts; and the Bacardi Building, Mexico City.

Visit http://www.greatbuildings.com /architects/Ludwig_Mies_van_der_ Rohe.html to learn more about his career and view photographs of some of the buildings he designed.

Reach for the Sky

The word *skyscraper* is used to describe any habitable building that is more than 500 feet tall. Below is a list of the world's 10 tallest buildings, according to the Council on Tall Buildings and Urban Habitat (http://www.ctbuh.org). Height is measured in feet from the sidewalk level of the main entrance to the structural top of the building. Antennas and flagpoles are not included.

1. Burj Khalifa
   Dubai, United Arab Emirates
   2,717 feet, 162 floors
2. Taipei 101
   Taipei, Taiwan
   1,667 feet, 101 stories
3. Shanghai World Financial Center
   Shanghai, China
   1,614 feet, 101 stories
4. Petronas Twin Towers
   Kuala Lumpur, Malaysia
   1,483 feet, 88 stories
5. Willis Tower
   Chicago, United States
   1,451 feet, 108 stories
6. Trump International Hotel & Tower
   Chicago, United States
   1,389 feet, 98 stories
7. Jin Mao Building
   Shanghai, China
   1,380 feet, 88 stories
8. Two International Finance Centre
   Hong Kong, China
   1,352 feet, 88 stories
9. CITIC Plaza
   Guangzhou, China
   1,280 feet, 80 stories
10. Shun Hing Square
    Shenzhen, China
    1,260 feet, 69 stories

Earnings

Newly licensed architects started at about $41,320 a year in 2008, according to the U.S. Department of Labor. Most architects earn between $53,000 and $91,000 a year. Architects who are partners in architectural firms or who have their own

FOR MORE INFO

For information on careers and schools, contact
American Institute of Architects
1735 New York Avenue, NW
Washington, DC 20006-5292
800-AIA-3837
infocentral@aia.org
http://www.aia.org

For information on careers and membership for high school students, contact
American Institute of Architecture Students
1735 New York Avenue, NW
Washington, DC 20006-5292

202-626-7472
mailbox@aias.org
http://www.aias.org

For information on architecture schools, contact
Association of Collegiate Schools of Architecture
1735 New York Avenue, NW
Washington, DC 20006-5292
202-785-2324
http://www.acsa-arch.org

businesses earn more than $119,000 a year. Partners in some very large firms make more than $130,000.

Outlook

Employment for architects is expected to be good during the next decade. Despite this prediction, competition will be strong for jobs. Many people want to enter this field. On the positive side, employment of architects is not likely to be affected by the growing use of computer technologies. Rather than replacing architects, computers are being used to make their jobs easier.

One major area of growth for architects is "green" design, also known as sustainable architecture. In this specialty, architects create environmentally friendly designs for buildings that save energy, use renewable resources (like the Sun and the wind), and use "green" building materials.

Astronomers

What Astronomers Do

Have you ever looked up at the night sky and wondered how the stars and Moon were formed and why the sky changes over time? If so, there might be a career in astronomy in your future.

Astronomers study the universe and all its celestial, or cosmic, bodies. They use telescopes, computers, and complex measuring tools to find the positions of stars and planets. They calculate the orbits of comets, asteroids, and artificial satellites. They study how celestial objects form and deteriorate. They try to figure out how the universe started.

With special equipment, astronomers collect and analyze information about planets and stars, such as temperature, shape, size, brightness, and motion. They try to explain how the universe came to exist, how elements formed, why galaxies look the way they do, and whether there is other life in the universe.

Because the field of astronomy is so broad, astronomers usually focus on one area of study. For example, *stellar astronomers* study the stars. *Solar astronomers* study the Sun. *Planetary astronomers* study conditions on the planets. *Cosmologists* study the origin and the structure of the universe, and *astrophysicists* study the physical and chemical changes that happen in the universe. *Celestial mechanics specialists* study the motion and position of planets and other objects in the solar system. *Radio astronomers* study the source and nature of celestial radio waves using sensitive radio telescopes.

Most astronomers teach at universities or colleges. A few lecture at planetariums and teach classes for the public. Some

EXPLORING

- Read books about astronomy. Here are a few suggestions: *Astronomy: Out of This World!*, by Dan Green (Kingfisher, 2009); *The Manga Guide to the Universe,* by Ishikawa Kenji (No Starch Press, 2010); and *George's Secret Key to the Universe* and *George's Cosmic Treasure Hunt,* both by Stephen and Lucy Hawking (Simon & Schuster Children's Publishing, 2009).

- There are many astronomy sites on the Internet. The National Aeronautics and Space Administration (NASA) has a Web site especially for kids. You can learn about Earth and the other planets, space travel, the stars and galaxies, and NASA. You can even watch exciting videos of astronauts and spaceships. Here is the address: http://www.nasa.gov/audience/forkids/home. Here are a few more Web site suggestions: A New Universe to Discover: Careers in Astronomy (http://aas.org/education/careers.php), Intro to Astronomy (http://www.astronomy.com/asy/default.aspx?c=ps&id=6), Ask the Space Scientist (http://image.gsfc.nasa.gov/poetry/ask/askmag.html), Astronomy Today (http://www.astronomy-today.com), and Space Weather.com (http://www.space-weather.com).

- Join an amateur astronomy club. There are many such clubs all over the country. These clubs usually have telescopes and will let members of the public view the night sky.

- Visit a nearby planetarium and ask astronomers who work there about their jobs. Planetariums also help you learn more about the universe and see if this is a career you would like.

- Ask a counselor or teacher to help arrange an informational interview with an astronomer. Ask the following questions: What made you want to enter this career? What are your main and secondary job duties? What do you like least and most about your job?

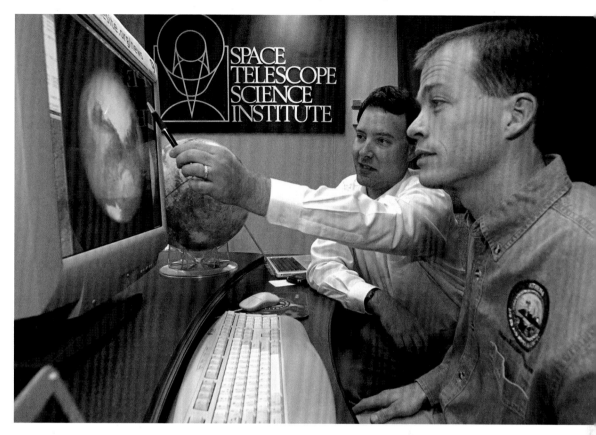

Astronomers study photographs of the planet Mars that were taken by the Hubble Space Telescope. (Gail Burton, AP Photo)

work at research institutions or at observatories. Those who work at observatories spend three to six nights a month observing the night sky through a telescope. They spend the rest of their time in offices or laboratories where they study, analyze their data, and write reports. Other astronomers work for government agencies or private industry.

Education and Training

You can begin training to become an astronomer in high school. You should plan to take classes in math, chemistry, physics, geography, and foreign languages (especially French, German, and

DID YOU KNOW?

- The Earth is about 93 million miles away from the Sun. It is the third planet from the Sun.
- Our Sun is so large that you could fit 1 million Earths inside.
- The Moon is just one-quarter the size of Earth.
- The Moon has a wide range of temperature extremes. In the daytime, its mean temperature is 225°F. At night, its mean temperature is -243°F.
- Asteroids can be as tiny as a pebble. The largest known asteroid is Ceres. It is about 580 miles in diameter.

Source: Astronomy.com

Russian). Because astronomy is a high-technology field, you should try to learn as much as you can about computers.

After high school you will have to earn a bachelor's degree in physics, mathematics, or astronomy. Once you receive your bachelor's degree, you may find work as an assistant or researcher. Most astronomers go on to earn both a master's degree and a doctorate.

Earnings

Astronomers had average earnings of $101,300 in 2008, according to the U.S. Department of Labor. Salaries ranged from less than $45,000 to $156,000 or more annually. The average for astronomers employed by the federal government was $124,810.

Will Asteroids Strike Earth?

Earth and all the other planets and moons have been continuously hit by asteroids and comets. Craters on Earth's moon are evidence of those strikes. Some people believe an asteroid or comet could strike the Earth and cause a disaster. But how likely is this? Astronomers and other scientists say such an event is not very likely. The most dangerous asteroids, those capable of causing major disasters, are extremely rare, according to NASA. These objects hit Earth once every 100,000 years on average.

FOR MORE INFO

Visit the FAQ section at the following Web site to read the online article "Career Profile: Astronomy."
American Association of Amateur Astronomers
PO Box 7981
Dallas, TX 75209-0981
aaaa@astromax.com
http://www.astromax.com

To read *A New Universe to Discover: A Guide to Careers in Astronomy,* visit the society's Web site.
American Astronomical Society
2000 Florida Avenue, NW, Suite 400
Washington, DC 20009-1231

202-328-2010
aas@aas.org
http://www.aas.org

This organization is a resource for professionals who work in many physics disciplines, including astronomy. For more information, contact
American Institute of Physics
One Physics Ellipse
College Park, MD 20740-3843
301-209-3100
aipinfo@aip.org
http://www.aip.org

Outlook

Astronomy is one of the smallest science fields, so people trained in astronomy must compete with many others for the best jobs. Many astronomers find jobs in universities and government agencies. Job opportunities are expected to be good in these settings. Astronomy graduates with just a bachelor's degree will find it hard to get top research positions. Instead, they can find work as high school science teachers or work as science technicians in private industry.

Bank Services Workers

What Bank Services Workers Do

You probably have seen a bank services worker when you've visited a bank with your parents. But what do these workers do and what exactly is a bank?

A bank receives, exchanges, lends, and safeguards money. Bank services workers handle money. There are many types of workers employed in the banking industry.

Bank tellers handle certain types of customer account transactions. These employees serve the public directly. They accept customers' deposits and give them receipts (a record of their transaction). They also pay out withdrawals, record transactions, and cash checks. In addition, they make sure that there is enough money in the customer's account to cover the check.

Bank clerks keep the vast amounts of paperwork and the computerized records in a bank in order. They keep track of deposit slips, checks, financial statements, and letters and emails sent by customers

EXPLORING

- Visit the following Web sites to learn more about money and financial management: Kids & Money (http://www.ext.nodak.edu/extnews/pipeline/d-parent.htm) and Investing for Kids (http://library.thinkquest.org/3096).
- Read books and magazines about the banking industry and financial topics.
- Volunteer to be the banker when you play games like Monopoly.
- Ask your parents to teach you how to write checks and how to use a checkbook.
- Ask your parents to help you open your own bank account.
- Talk to a bank services worker about his or her career.

or other banks. They record transactions and file records. They may assist customers, answer telephone calls and emails, and do other general duties.

Bank officers and managers supervise workers and handle loans and other financial matters at a bank. They direct employees, make assignments, and oversee day-to-day operations. Bank officers might also work in accounting, public relations, advertising, or other areas of a bank. Officers review budgets and other financial records. A manager or officer must research what other local banks are doing and how strong the economy is. If the economy is strong, many people have jobs and money to spend or save. If the economy is poor, fewer people have jobs or money

A bank teller makes change for a customer. (Bob Daemmrich, The Image Works)

Tips for Success

To be a successful bank services worker, you should

- be outgoing and friendly
- be able to handle occasional unhappy or angry customers
- be honest and accurate
- pay close attention to detail
- have a good understanding of financial matters

to save or spend. These factors will influence what services the bank's customers will want. The bank officer usually prepares daily or weekly reports for the bank president.

Education and Training

Most banks prefer that bank clerks and tellers have completed high school. Employers look for applicants who have taken courses in bookkeeping, typing, business, and mathematics. You should also be able to operate business machines, including computers.

Bank officers and managers need to understand finances, economics, and the rules and regulations of the banking industry. To become a bank officer or manager, you will need a bachelor's degree in economics, accounting, finance, or business administration. A growing number of banks want their bank officers and managers to have master's degrees.

DID YOU KNOW?

The first automatic teller machine (ATM) was installed at Citizens and Southern National Bank in Valdosta, Georgia, in 1970. Today, you can find ATMs everywhere.

Earnings

Bank tellers earned an average salary of $23,610 a year in 2008, according to the U.S. Department of Labor. Clerks' salaries ranged from less than $17,000 to $31,000 or more per year. Bank officers and managers had median salaries of $99,330 in 2008. Very experienced officers and managers earned $135,000 or more a year.

FOR MORE INFO

For information on money management for people of all ages, contact
American Bankers Association
1120 Connecticut Avenue, NW
Washington, DC 20036-3902
800-226-5377
http://www.aba.com

For industry information, contact
Bank Administration Institute
115 South LaSalle Street, Suite 3300
Chicago, IL 60603-3801
888-284-4078
info@bai.org
http://www.bai.org

Outlook

Employment opportunities are expected to be favorable for bank services workers. The growing number of bank branches (including those at grocery stores), together with longer hours and more services offered to draw in more customers, will require more tellers. There should be many jobs for clerks and related workers. People constantly leave this career field because the lower level jobs do not pay a lot. Mergers and closings may limit the number of new positions available for bank officers and managers. They will still be needed to help banks face greater competition, to handle changing tax laws, and to help banks comply with stricter record-keeping policies.

Bioinformatics Specialists

What Bioinformatics Specialists Do

Bioinformatics specialists collect, manage, and study biological (especially DNA) and biochemical data at the molecular level by using computer software and hardware. Bioinformatics is used to develop new ways to study, diagnose, and treat genetic diseases such as muscular dystrophy, family-linked cancers, and Huntington's disease. It is also used to help reduce the time it takes to develop new drugs (such as those that fight AIDS) and in many other medical applications. Bioinformatics specialists are also known as *biostatisticians, computational biologists,* and *biometricians.*

To conduct research, bioinformatics specialists design computer databases and develop complicated mathematical formulas called algorithms to gather and analyze biological and biochemical information. These algorithms allow them to identify major risk factors for cancer, lung disease, and heart disease, among other conditions. They can also be used to determine the role environmental factors such as tobacco smoke or pollutants have on overall human health.

Bioinformatics specialists are employed by government, medical, and academic research laboratories; the pharmaceutical and biotechnology industries; computer hardware and software companies that serve bioinformatics-related industries; and health informatics companies. They also work as researchers and teachers at colleges and universities.

Tips for Success

To be a successful bioinformatics specialist, you should

- have excellent computer skills
- be very knowledgeable about medical science
- have an analytical mind
- have patience
- have strong communication skills
- be highly ethical
- be able to work as a member of a team
- be willing to continue to learn throughout your career

Education and Training

In high school, take as many science (especially biology and chemistry), math, and computer science (especially database design) courses as possible. English and speech classes will help you to develop your communication skills, which are important for success in this field.

A bachelor's degree in biostatistics or bioinformatics is necessary to work as a bioinformatics specialist. Some students combine a degree in statistics with minor in biology, chemistry, or a related field. Many people go on to earn graduate degrees in biostatistics or bioinformatics. Typical courses in bioinformatics programs include cell and molecular biology, genetics, bioethics, biostatistical methods, data analysis, calculus, statistics, computer science, database design, and chemistry. In addition

Math Whizzes

- Maria Gaetana Agnesi (1718–99) was known for her discussion of the cubic curve and was called the Witch of Agnesi.
- Archimedes (c. 287–212 B.C.) was a Greek mathematician and inventor known for his work in mechanics and hydrostatics.
- Euclid (c. 300 B.C.) was a Greek geometer (a practitioner of geometry) whose main work, *Elements,* was a chief source of geometrical reasoning and methods until the 19th century.
- Sophie Germain (1776–1831) was a French mathematician who contributed to the study of acoustics and elasticity and the theory of numbers.

Source: *Funk & Wagnalls New Encyclopedia*

to classwork, students spend a considerable amount of time in computer and science laboratories. One or more internships are typically required.

Earnings

The U.S. Department of Labor reports that the median annual salary for biological scientists (including bioinformatics specialists) was $65,080 in 2008. Those just starting out in the field earned less than $35,000. Scientists with a lot of experience earned more than $101,000. Those who worked for the federal government earned a mean annual salary of $70,270. Bioinformatics specialists with advanced degrees earn the highest salaries.

Outlook

Employment is expected to be excellent for bioinformatics specialists during the next decade. The completion of the Human

FOR MORE INFO

For information on bioinformatics, contact the following organizations:

American Institute of Biological Sciences
1444 I Street, NW, Suite 200
Washington, DC 20005-6535
202-628-1500
http://www.aibs.org

American Society for Biochemistry and Molecular Biology
9650 Rockville Pike
Bethesda, MD 20814-3996
301-634-7145
asbmb@asbmb.org
http://www.asbmb.org

American Society for Microbiology
1752 N Street, NW
Washington, DC 20036-2904

202-737-3600
http://www.asm.org

Bioinformatics Organization
http://www.bioinformatics.org

Biotechnology Industry Organization
1201 Maryland Avenue, SW, Suite 900
Washington, DC 20024-2149
202-962-9200
info@bio.org
http://www.bio.org

International Society for Computational Biology
Pharmaceutical Sciences Building, Room 3230
9500 Gilman Drive, MC 0743
La Jolla, CA 92093-0743
http://www.iscb.org

Genome Project has allowed scientists to compile a vast amount of genetic information. This will create strong demand for bioinformatics specialists to help gather, study, and utilize this information for the good of society. Bioinformatics specialists with advanced degrees will have the best employment prospects.

Bookkeepers

What Bookkeepers Do

Bookkeepers keep records of the finances of companies and other organizations. They may record these transactions in an account book or on a computer. From time to time, they prepare statements that summarize the funds received and paid out. Bookkeepers use a variety of tools in their work. These include computers, software spreadsheet programs, fax machines, photocopiers, scanners, calculators, and references such as yearly tax guides.

Bookkeeping records are very important to any company. They show how much money the company has and how much it owes. They also show how much money the company has earned or lost in a certain period of time. Bookkeeping records are especially important when a company submits income tax reports to the federal government and profit and loss reports to company owners. (A profit report details the amount of money a company earned after expenses; a loss report details the amount of money the company lost.)

EXPLORING

- Keep an account of your own finances. Write down your income, including your allowance, gifts, or money you earn for odd jobs or babysitting. Keep track of your expenses—food and drink, clothing, music and movies, and so on.
- Volunteer to be the treasurer for school clubs.
- Use your school's resource center or local library to find computer software designed for money management.
- Talk to a bookkeeper about his or her career.

A Career in Bookkeeping:
The Good News and the Bad News

What's the good news?

- Flexible hours
- Both part-time and full-time jobs are available
- You can work independently

What's the downside of bookkeeping jobs?

- Sometimes repetitive tasks
- Deadlines
- Government reporting

Bookkeepers work for a wide variety of employers. These range from small businesses to large corporations to government agencies. For example, bookkeepers may work for factories, stores, schools, banks, state financial agencies, insurance companies, hotels, or railroads.

General bookkeepers usually work for small businesses. They may do all the tasks involved in keeping a complete set of bookkeeping records. They use adding machines, calculators, and computers (including software programs). They may also do other types of office work, such as filing papers and answering telephone calls or emails.

In large businesses, an accountant may supervise the workers in the bookkeeping department. These workers sometimes are called *accounting clerks.* They usually do specialized tasks. Some record items in account books and make out bills. Others prepare reports, write checks, or make payroll lists.

Bookkeepers need strong mathematical skills. They must be organized and able to concentrate on detailed work. The work is often repetitive, and bookkeepers should not mind sitting for long hours behind a desk. They should be methodical, accurate, and orderly and enjoy working on detailed tasks. Employers look for honest and trustworthy people, because they are placing their business in the bookkeeper's hands.

Education and Training

Bookkeepers must have at least a high school education. Employers prefer to hire those who have taken business-related courses in high school. Such courses include math, bookkeeping, and computer science. Some employers look for people who have completed a junior college or business school training program. Others offer on-the-job training to workers.

Some schools and employers participate in work-study programs. In these programs, students work at part-time bookkeeping jobs. They also are required to attend class and complete class assignments.

Earnings

Earnings for bookkeepers vary based on the size of the city where they work and the size and type of business that employs them. According to the U.S. Department of Labor, bookkeep-

Profile: Blaise Pascal (1623–62)

Blaise Pascal was a French mathematician, physicist, and philosopher. He is credited with inventing one of the first mechanical calculators, the arithmetical triangle, and the hydraulic press. Along with Pierre de Fermat, he founded the modern theory of probability. Probability is the likelihood that something will happen. Mathematical computations are used to determine probability.

In honor of Pascal's groundbreaking work, the computer scientist Nicklaus Wirth named his new computer language Pascal in 1972.

Sources: About.com

FOR MORE INFO

Visit the institute's Web site for information on certification and tips and advice for bookkeepers.
American Institute of Professional Bookkeepers
6001 Montrose Road, Suite 500
Rockville, MD 20852-4873
800-622-0121
info@aipb.org
http://www.aipb.org

For information on women in accounting, contact
Educational Foundation for Women in Accounting
136 South Keowee Street
Dayton, OH 45402-2241
937-424-3391
info@efwa.org
http://www.efwa.org

ers earned a median annual income of $32,510 a year in 2008. Clerks just starting out earned approximately $21,000 in 2008. Those with one or two years of college generally earned higher starting wages. Top-paying jobs averaged $49,000 or more.

Outlook

More than 2 million people work in bookkeeping jobs. Employment of bookkeepers and accounting clerks is expected to be good during the next decade. Most job openings will be created as workers retire or change jobs. New jobs will become available as smaller businesses and industries expand. The use of computers makes the bookkeeper's job easier, but it also means that businesses need fewer bookkeepers to do the same amount of work.

Computer Systems Analysts

What Computer Systems Analysts Do

Computer systems analysts help banks, government offices, and businesses understand their computer systems. Most organizations use computers to store data. They need analysts who can design computer systems and programs for the specific needs of a business, or even to the needs of just one department in a business.

Computer systems analysts work with both the hardware and software parts of computer systems. Hardware includes the large items such as the computer itself, the monitor, and the keyboard. Software includes the computer programs, which are written and stored on disks, and the documentation (the manuals or guidebooks) that goes with the programs. Analysts design the best mix of hardware and software for the needs of the company that employs them.

A computer systems analyst for the personnel department of a large company, for example, would first talk to the department manager about which areas of the business could be helped by computer technology. If the company started a new policy of giving employees longer paid vacations at Christmas, the manager might want to know how this policy has affected company profits for the month of December. The analyst can show the manager what computer program to use, what data to enter, and how to read the charts or graphs that the computer produces. The work of the analyst allows the manager to review the raw data. In this case, the numbers show that company profits were the same as in the previous Decembers.

EXPLORING

- Visit the Association for Computing Machinery's career Web site, http://computing-careers.acm.org, for information on career paths, a list of suggested high school classes, profiles of computer science students, and answers to frequently asked questions about the field.
- Read books about computers and careers in the field. Here are some suggestions: *Careers for Computer Buffs & Other Technological Types*, 3rd edition, by Marjorie Eberts (McGraw-Hill, 2006); *The Complete Idiot's Guide to Computer Basics*, 5th edition, by Joe Kraynak (Alpha, 2009); *Absolute Beginner's Guide to Computer Basics*, 5th edition, by Michael Miller (Que Publishing, 2009); and *How Computers Work*, 9th edition, by Ron White and Timothy Edward Downs (Que Publishing, 2007).
- Play strategy games, such as chess. Such games are a good way to use analytic thinking skills while having fun. Commercial games range in themes from war simulations to world historical development.
- Learn everything you can about computers. Work and play with them on a daily basis.
- Ask your teacher or counselor to help you set up an informational interview with a computer systems analyst.
- You might want to try hooking up a computer system at home or school, configuring terminals, printers, and modems. This activity requires a fair amount of knowledge and should be supervised by a parent.

The manager can then decide whether to continue the company policy.

Once analysts have the computer system set up and operating, they advise on equipment and programming changes. Often, people in a department each have their own computer,

Words to Learn

ASCII (American Standard Code for Information Exchange) numerical code used by personal computers

database a collection of information stored on a computer

debugging identifying and correcting errors in software

GUI (graphical user interface) a system that uses symbols (icons) seen on screen to represent available functions; pronounced "gooey"

hardware the physical components of a computer system; they typically include the motherboard, disk drives, display, keyboard, and the central processing unit

LAN (Local Area Network) a network that exists at one location, typically an office

network two or more computers that are electronically connected to share data and programs

software programs that tell computer hardware what to do and how to do it

spreadsheet a program that performs mathematical operations; used mainly for accounting and other record keeping

WAN (Wide Area Network) a network that includes remote sites in different buildings, cities, states, or countries

wireless network a telecommunications network that uses electromagnetic waves, rather than wires, to transmit information

but they must be able to connect with and use information from all the computers. Analysts must then work with all the different computers in a department or a company so the computers can connect with each other. This system of connected computers is called a network.

Systems analysts who conduct detailed testing of the systems they set up are called *software quality assurance analysts*. If they find a problem, they figure out what caused it and fix the problem.

Systems programmer-analysts are specialists who design and update software that is used in computer systems. They are often asked to write new software that solves a particular problem that the company has encountered.

To be a successful computer systems analyst, you should like to solve problems and know a lot about computer hardware and software. You should be able to work well with many types of people, from management to data entry clerks. You must be able to learn about new technology quickly. This field is constantly changing. Finally, you should have good time-management skills, be able to work as a member of a team, and be able to work under deadline pressure.

DID YOU KNOW?

Where Computer Systems Analysts Work

- Manufacturing companies
- Data processing service firms
- Hardware and software companies
- Banks
- Insurance companies
- Credit companies
- Publishing companies
- Government agencies
- Colleges and universities

Education and Training

Take advanced high school classes in math, science, and computer science to prepare for this work. Since analysts do a lot of proposal writing, it is a good idea to take English classes too. Speech classes will help prepare you for making formal presentations to management and clients.

To work as a computer systems analyst in a scientific or technical environment, you will need at least a bachelor's degree in computer science, applied mathematics, information science,

DID YOU KNOW?

- Approximately 532,000 computer systems analysts are employed in the United States. About 24 percent work in the computer systems design and related services industry.
- About 6 percent of computer systems analysts are self-employed.
- Some computer systems analysts work more than 50 hours a week.

Source: U.S. Department of Labor

engineering, or the physical sciences. Those who work for businesses usually have a degree in a business-related field such as management information systems. Analysts in highly technical areas (aeronautics, for example) usually have graduate degrees as well. Many employers are now seeking applicants with a master's degree in business administration with a concentration in information systems.

In addition to a college degree, job experience as a computer programmer is very helpful. Many businesses choose computer programmers already on staff and train them on the job to be systems analysts. Computer systems analysts with several years of experience are often promoted into managerial jobs.

Earnings

Starting salaries for computer systems analysts averaged about $45,000 a year in 2008, according to the U.S. Department of Labor. After several years of experience, analysts can earn $75,000 a year. Computer systems analysts with many years of experience and a master's degree can earn more than $118,000 a year. Salaries for analysts in government are somewhat lower than the average for private industry. Earnings also depend on years of experience and the type of business you work for.

Outlook

Employment for computer systems analysts will be excellent during the next decade. Businesses are using more computers,

FOR MORE INFO

For information on careers, contact
Association for Computing Machinery
2 Penn Plaza, Suite 701
New York, NY 10121-0701
800-342-6626
acmhelp@acm.org
http://www.acm.org

For information on career opportunities for women in computing, contact
Association for Women in Computing
41 Sutter Street, Suite 1006
San Francisco, CA 94104-4905
info@awc-hq.org
http://www.awc-hq.org

For information on professional development, contact
Association of Information Technology Professionals
401 North Michigan Avenue, Suite 2400
Chicago, IL 60611-4267

http://www.aitp.org

For information on computer careers and student programs, contact
IEEE Computer Society
1730 Massachusetts Avenue, NW
Washington, DC 20036-1992
202-371-0101
http://www.computer.org

For information on certification, contact
Institute for Certification of Computing Professionals
2350 East Devon Avenue, Suite 281
Des Plaines, IL 60018-4602
800-843-8227
office2@iccp.org
http://www.iccp.org

and they will rely more and more on systems analysts to make the right purchasing decisions and to keep systems running smoothly. There is also an increasing focus on computer security and networking new technologies into company networks. This will create new job opportunities for computer systems analysts.

Demographers

What Demographers Do

Demographers collect and study facts about a society's population. These facts include statistics on births, marriages, deaths, education, and income levels. Their population studies tell what the society is really like and help experts predict economic and social trends. For example, demographers may study birth rates of a community. They may find that the population of school-age children is growing faster than expected and that new schools will have to be built. Or demographers may collect facts about how many of these children have been sick with measles. These facts could be studied to find out how effective a measles vaccine is.

Demographers work for both government agencies and private companies. Local, state, and federal government agencies use demographers to help them provide enough of the right kinds of transportation, education, police, and health services. Private companies need demographers' collections of facts (statistics) to help them improve their products or services and predict who will buy them. For example, a retail chain might use a demographer's study to help decide the best location to open a new store. Demographers may also teach in colleges and universities or work as consultants for private companies or communities as a whole.

Demographers use computers to help them gather and analyze the millions of pieces of information they need to make their forecasts. It is up to the individual demographer to know how to read the statistics and put them together in a meaningful way. They also use geographic information systems (GIS) technology to do their work. GIS technology is basically a computer system that can assemble, store, manipulate, and display geographically referenced information.

An *applied statistician,* a specialized type of demographer, uses accepted theories and known statistical formulas to collect and analyze data in a specific area, such as the availability of health care in a specified location.

Tips for Success

To be a successful demographer, you should

- enjoy using logic to solve problems
- be good at math and using computers
- like detailed work
- be good at conducting research
- have excellent written and oral communication skills
- be ethical

Education and Training

Students interested in this field should have strong skills in numbers and mathematics, especially algebra and geometry. In high school, you should take classes in social studies, English, and math. Training in computer science also is especially helpful.

Demographers need a college degree in sociology or public health with special studies in demography. Many entry-level jobs require a master's degree. Some colleges offer master's degrees in demography. Typical courses in a graduate-level program include introduction to demography, demographic analysis, geographic information systems, forecasting, mathematical demography, and introduction to research methods.

As the field gets more competitive, many demographers (especially those who wish to work for the federal government) will earn a doctorate in demography or sociology. The most successful demographers specialize in one area. You must also keep up with advances in the field by continuing your education throughout your career.

Earnings

Earnings vary according to education, training, and place of employment. Salaries for social scientists (a group that includes

Profile: Joseph Adna Hill (1860–1938)

Joseph Adna Hill was an American statistician who had a long career with the U.S. Census Bureau. He began working as a statistician for the bureau in 1898 and became its chief statistician in 1909. As chief statistician, he supervised the publication of reports on women in the workforce, child labor, illiteracy, marriage and divorce, and the occupations of immigrants. In 1921, Hill became the assistant director of the bureau.

Hill is probably best known, along with the mathematician Edward Vermilye Huntington, for developing an algorithm (a mathematical formula) to apportion seats to the states in the U.S. House of Representatives. Seats are awarded based on the population of the state, which is updated every 10 years by the U.S. Census Bureau. For example, the state of New York receives more seats than the state of Montana because there are more people per square mile in New York. Accurate population statistics are necessary in planning immigration policies, public health programs, advertising and marketing campaigns, and other activities.

The algorithm Hill and Huntington developed is known as the Method of Equal Proportions or the Huntington-Hill method. It still used today to apportion seats in the U.S. House of Representatives.

Source: U.S. Census Bureau

FOR MORE INFO

For career publications and lists of accredited schools, contact

American Sociological Association
1430 K Street, NW, Suite 600
Washington, DC 20005-2529
202-383-9005
http://www.asanet.org

For information on publications, contact
Population Association of America
8630 Fenton Street, Suite 722
Silver Spring, MD 20910-3812
http://www.popassoc.org

For publications, special reports, and global population information, contact

Population Reference Bureau
1875 Connecticut Avenue, NW, Suite 520
Washington, DC 20009-5728
800-877-9881
popref@prb.org
http://www.prb.org

For population statistics and information about the U.S. Census Bureau, contact

U.S. Census Bureau
4600 Silver Hill Road
Washington, DC 20233-0001
301-763-4748
http://www.census.gov

demographers) ranged from less than $37,000 to more than $108,000 in 2008, according to the U.S. Department of Labor. The median annual salary for social scientists was $68,720.

Outlook

There is a large amount of fact-gathering and social science research going on in the United States. Trained demographers will be needed to conduct and study this research. Job opportunities will be greatest in and around large cities, because that is where many colleges, universities, and other research facilities are located. There may be an increasing demand for demographers in international organizations such as the World Bank, the United Nations, and the World Health Organization. Demographers in these organizations will be needed to help developing countries (those that do not have a lot of material wealth) analyze their own growing populations and plan for necessary services.

Economists

What Economists Do

We all make decisions on how to spend money, but *economists* do so on a large scale. They work with companies and the government to help plan various programs and projects. Economists research how people spend their money and what goods and services are being produced.

Many economists work for businesses to help plan what products to make or services to offer and how much to charge. An economist may study such factors as how many potential customers there are in a certain area, how much they pay for a product or service, and which other companies are selling the product or service. Economists also study statistics showing how much a product costs to make and where the manufacturer should invest its profits (the money it earns after expenses). Economists analyze these factors and then report their findings to management officials. This information is used in future planning.

Economists collect and analyze the appropriate statistics and examine how various numbers are related. For example, an economist

An economist talks about the current state of the petroleum industry during a press conference. (Gerald Herbert, AP Photo)

may find that salaries are going up and use that information to explain, in part, why prices for products or services are also increasing.

Economists usually specialize in a specific branch of their field. *Government economists* look at larger issues than those who work for private companies. Their conclusions may affect governmental policy. A *labor economist* for the government may investigate salaries paid to workers across the country and how many people are working nationwide. They use this information to determine and report various economic trends. *International economists* study how many local goods are sold to foreign

Tips for Success

To be a successful economist, you should

- be good at math
- have good computer skills
- be detail oriented
- enjoy doing research
- have great communication skills
- be able to explain your findings and theories to people from all different backgrounds
- be willing to continue to learn throughout your career

DID YOU KNOW?

- There are about 14,600 economists employed in the United States.
- Thirty-one percent work for the federal government and 22 percent work in state and local government agencies.
- Employment of economists is expected to grow by 6 percent from 2008 to 2018, or slower than the average growth for all careers.

Source: U.S. Department of Labor

countries and how many foreign goods are bought here. They study statistics to make sure that their government is benefiting from its exchange of goods with other nations. *Financial economists* study credit, money, and other statistics and trends to help develop public policy. *Industrial economists* study the way businesses are organized and suggest ways to use profits or other assets. *Environmental economists* study the links between economic issues and the distribution and management of natural resources. *Agricultural economists* study food production, development in rural areas, and the distribution of natural resources.

Many economists work as researchers at government agencies, such as the U.S. Department of Labor, or international organizations, such as the United Nations. Others teach at colleges and universities. Still others find employment at nonprofit or for-profit organizations, helping these organizations determine how to use their resources or grow in profitability. Most economics-related positions are concentrated in large cities, although academic positions are spread throughout the United States.

FOR MORE INFO

For information on agricultural economics and a list of colleges that offer programs in the field, contact
Agricultural and Applied Economics Association
555 East Wells Street, Suite 1100
Milwaukee, WI 53202-3800
414-918-3190
info@aaea.org
http://www.aaea.org

For general information about economics, contact
American Economic Association
2014 Broadway, Suite 305
Nashville, TN 37203-2425
615-322-2595
info@econlit.org
http://www.aeaweb.org

For information on graduate programs in environmental and resource economics, contact
Association of Environmental and Resource Economists
1616 P Street, NW, Room 600
Washington, DC 20036-1434

202-328-5125
http://www.aere.org

The council promotes the economic education of students from kindergarten through 12th grade. It offers teacher training courses and materials. For more information, contact
Council for Economic Education
122 East 42 Street, Suite 2600
New York, NY 10168-2699
800-338-1192
http://www.councilforeconed.org

For information on careers, contact
National Association for Business Economics
1233 20th Street, NW, Suite 505
Washington, DC 20036-2365
202-463-6223
nabe@nabe.com
http://www.nabe.com

For industry information, contact
Society of Government Economists
PO Box 77082
Washington, DC 20013-8082
http://www.sge-econ.org

Education and Training

In high school, take courses in mathematics, English, and writing, and any available classes in economics or other social sciences. Computers are important in all types of statistical work, so make sure to take computer classes, particularly those that teach spreadsheet and database programs.

A bachelor's degree with a major in economics or business administration is the minimum requirement for an entry-level position such as research assistant or marketing, finance, or sales worker. The federal government requires candidates for entry-level economist positions to have a minimum of 21 semester hours of economics and three hours of statistics, accounting, or calculus, or a combination of experience and education. A master's degree, or even a Ph.D. in economics, is more commonly required for most positions as an economist.

Earnings

Economists earned a median annual salary of $83,590 in 2008, according to the U.S. Department of Labor. Those just starting out in the field earned less than $44,000. Economists with advanced degrees and experience earned $149,000 or more annually. Economists who were employed by the federal government earned an average salary of $108,010.

Outlook

Employment opportunities for economists should be only fair during the next decade. Many economists work for government agencies, and jobs in this sector are declining.

Economists will find the best opportunities in private industry, especially in management, scientific, and technical consulting services.

Those who meet state certification requirements for teaching may wish to become secondary-school economics teachers. Demand for high school economics teachers is expected to increase.

People with a background in economics will be able to find better opportunities in related careers such as market analyst, financial analyst, public policy consultant, researcher or research assistant, and purchasing manager.

Engineers and Engineering Technicians

What Engineers and Engineering Technicians Do

Engineers, more than any other professionals, are responsible for discoveries and inventions that are part of our everyday lives. They use scientific knowledge and tools to design products, structures, and machines. Most engineers specialize in a particular area. *Electrical and electronic engineers,* for example, work in the medical, computer, missile guidance, and power distribution fields. Engineers have a wide range of choices in the type of work they want to do.

A nuclear power station is a good example of how different engineering specialties work together. *Civil engineers* help select the site for the power station. They draw blueprints (mathematical plans) for all structural details of the building. *Nuclear engineers* handle every stage of the production of nuclear energy, from processing nuclear fuels to the disposal of radioactive wastes. *Environmental engineers* also find ways to safely dispose of such wastes. *Mechanical engineers* design and build engines that use nuclear fuel to produce power. *Electrical engineers* and *computer engineers* design equipment to distribute the electricity to thousands of customers. The device workers wear to detect the levels of radiation their bodies absorb over a period of time was developed by *biomedical engineers.*

Other major engineering specialties include: aerospace and aeronautical, agricultural, architectural, automotive, ceramic, chemical, electronics, fiber optics, fire protection, hardware,

EXPLORING

- Ask your librarian to help you find books and magazines about engineering and careers in engineering technology.
- Visit the Junior Engineering Technical Society's Web site (http://www.jets.org) for information about engineering careers, competitions, and programs.
- Join science and math clubs at your school.
- Work on science projects that involve inventing and building. Enter a project in a science fair.

- Try to visit a variety of different kinds of engineering facilities—service shops, manufacturing plants, and research laboratories—either through individual visits or through field trips organized by teachers or guidance counselors. These visits will give you a realistic idea of the opportunities in the different areas of the industry.
- Talk to engineers and engineering technicians about their careers.

health and safety, industrial, manufacturing, marine, materials, metallurgical, mining and geological, ocean, optical, packaging, petroleum, plastics, quality control, robotics, software, soils, and transportation.

There are about 1.6 million engineers in the United States. All engineers, whatever their specialty, have a strong math and science background and an ability to develop solutions to practical problems. All engineers are problem solvers and inventors. They all do highly technical work. They must have strong knowledge of how things work, from electronics to the human body, in order to come up with better ways of doing things.

Engineering technicians use engineering, science, and mathematics to help engineers and other professionals in research and development, quality control, manufacturing, and many other fields. Some major technician specialties include chemical, civil, electrical and electronics, industrial, and mechanical engineering.

Education and Training

Take a great deal of math in high school, including geometry, trigonometry, calculus, and two years of algebra. You should

Engineers run a test on bolts at Dana Corporation's Automotive Technology Center, where the company conducts research, development, and testing for future products. (Jim West Photography)

also develop a strong background in physics, chemistry, biology, and computer programming or applications. Because engineers must communicate constantly with other engineers, scientists, clients, and consumers, English and speech classes are important.

Engineers all have at least a four-year degree that gives them a clear understanding of how math and science applies to the everyday world. Most engineering degrees are in electrical, mechanical, or civil engineering. Graduates of these programs may then choose to further specialize in their area of interest by taking more college courses, earning a graduate degree, or getting on-the-job training. For example, a mechanical engineer who wants to work with nuclear reactors may study nuclear science beyond the undergraduate level or may take an entry-level engineering job at a nuclear plant before working up to becoming an actual nuclear engineer.

While some current engineering technicians enter the field without formal academic training, it is increasingly difficult to do so. Most employers are interested in hiring graduates with at least a two-year degree in engineering technology. Technical institutes, community colleges, vocational schools, and universities all offer this course of study.

Some engineering technicians decide to pursue advancement in their field by becoming engineering technologists. Others decide to branch off into research and development or become engineers. These higher level and higher paid positions typi-

Tips for Success

To be a successful engineer or engineering technician, you should

- like solving problems
- have a strong interest and ability in science and mathematics
- enjoy designing things
- be able to work as a member of a team and alone, as necessary
- have excellent communication skills
- be willing to continue to learn throughout your career

cally require the completion of a bachelor's degree in engineering technology (for engineering technologists) or at least a bachelor's degree in engineering (for technicians interested in research and development and aspiring engineers).

Earnings

Engineers are paid well for their work. Their salaries are among the highest starting salaries of any career. According to the National Association of Colleges and Employers, new engineers with bachelor's degrees averaged $43,000 to $61,000 a year in July 2009, depending on their specialty. Those with master's degrees and no experience averaged $52,000 to $83,000 a year. Engineers with several years of experience and education earned $130,000 or more a year.

The earnings of engineering technicians vary widely depending on skills and experience, the type of work, geographical location, and other factors. Salaries ranged from less than $26,000 to $82,000 or more annually in 2008.

Outlook

Engineers have great job security. Their work is necessary for maintaining and improving our way of life. Even when the economy is not healthy, engineers' jobs are generally safe. Demand will continue to be strong for engineers with a solid math and science background

DID YOU KNOW?

- There are about 1.6 million engineers employed in the United States.
- Thirty-six percent of engineers work in manufacturing industries; 30 percent in professional, scientific, and technical services industries; 6 percent for the federal government (primarily in the U.S. Departments of Agriculture, Defense, Energy, Interior, and Transportation, and in the National Aeronautics and Space Administration); and 6 percent for state and local governments (often in highway and public works departments).
- About 3 percent of engineers are self-employed.
- There are approximately 497,300 engineering technicians in the United States. The most popular engineering technician specialties are electrical and electronics (33 percent of all engineering technicians), civil (18 percent), industrial (15 percent), mechanical (9 percent), and environmental (4 percent).

Source: U.S. Department of Labor

FOR MORE INFO

For information on engineering associations, contact

American Association of Engineering Societies
6522 Meadowridge Road, Suite 101
Elkridge, MD 21075-6191
202-296-2237
http://www.aaes.org

For more information on careers in engineering, contact

American Society for Engineering Education
1818 N Street, NW, Suite 600
Washington, DC 20036-2479
202-331-3500
http://www.asee.org

For industry information, contact

American Society of Certified Engineering Technicians
PO Box 1536
Brandon, MS 39043-1536

601-824-8991
http://www.ascet.org

For information on engineering careers and students clubs and competitions, contact

Junior Engineering Technical Society
1420 King Street, Suite 405
Alexandria, VA 22314-2750
703-548-5387
info@jets.org
http://www.jets.org

For information on licensure and practice areas, contact

National Society of Professional Engineers
1420 King Street
Alexandria, VA 22314-2750
703-684-2800
http://www.nspe.org

and training in new technologies. Job opportunities will be best for biomedical, civil, environmental, industrial, mining/geological, and petroleum engineers.

Employment of engineering technicians is expected to be fair. Computer-aided design allows individual technicians to get more work done in less time, which limits job growth. Technicians with training in sophisticated technologies and those with degrees in technology will have the best employment opportunities. Opportunities will be best for civil and environmental engineering technicians.

Financial Planners

What Financial Planners Do

Financial planners, also known as *personal financial advisers,* advise their clients on many aspects of finance. They do not work alone. Financial planners meet with their clients' other advisers, such as attorneys, accountants, trust officers, and investment bankers. This helps financial planners understand their clients' overall finances. After meeting with the clients and their other advisers, financial planners analyze the information and write a report. This report lists the clients' financial objectives, current income, investments, expenses, tax returns, insurance, retirement programs, estate plans, and other important information. The report also includes recommendations on how the clients can best achieve their financial goals.

Financial planning is an ongoing process. The plan must be reviewed often so that changes can be made, if necessary, to make sure that it continues to meet the client's needs.

EXPLORING

- Check out the financial planning information available on the Internet to familiarize yourself with the terms used in the industry. Visit these Web sites: Investing for Kids (http://library.thinkquest.org/3096), U. S. Mint H.I.P. Pocket Change (http://www.usmint.gov/kids), and Kids' Finance (http://www.kidsfinance.com).
- Take as many finance and business classes as possible.
- If you live near a stock exchange, go for a visit. Most exchanges have their own Web sites.
- Talk to certified financial planners to learn more about the career.

DID YOU KNOW?

- The first American colonists used English, French, and Spanish money. In 1775, just before the Revolutionary War, the Continental Congress issued money to pay for the war. The first plates for this currency were made by Paul Revere, a silversmith and American patriot.
- The 1792 Mint Act established the coin system, with the dollar as the main unit.
- The United States became the first country in the world to use the decimal system for currency.
- The first coins—11,178 copper cents—were made in March 1793 at the Philadelphia Mint.
- The first paper money issued by the government was "demand notes," nicknamed "greenbacks."

Since they handle all of the money and investments that people have worked a lifetime to earn, financial planners must be ready to answer difficult questions about the plans they write.

People need financial planners for different things. Some might want life insurance, college savings plans, or estate planning. Sometimes these needs are caused by changes in people's lives, such as retirement, death of a spouse, disability, marriage, birth of children, or job changes. Financial planners spend most of their time on investment planning, retirement planning, tax planning, estate planning, and risk management. All of these areas require different types of financial knowledge.

For example, financial planners who are *retirement counselors* look at whether the client will be happy with simple living when he or she retires, or want to travel the world first class. Other issues must be addressed, such as relocation costs (the amount of money it will take to move to another city, perhaps in a warmer climate) or medical insurance needs. They must know about traditional sources of retirement funds, such as Social Security, personal savings, employer-sponsored plans, post-retirement employment, and inheritance (the passing on of money or property after an individual dies). Another retirement issue is the possibility of disability and the need for chronic illness care. Retirement planners may suggest disability income insurance, long-term care insurance, or a medical savings account as a precaution for such situations.

Words to Learn

assets resources that have monetary value, including cash, inventory, real estate, machinery, collectibles, and securities; **current assets** are those that can be converted to cash within a year; a **fixed asset** is a long-term asset, such as a building, piece of land, or patent (a legally registered invention or discovery) that will not be converted to cash within a year

commission-only a method of payment for financial planners; payment is received from the sale of financial products that clients agree to buy; there is no charge for advice or preparation of the financial plan

current liabilities debts that must be paid within a year

fee-only a method of payment for financial planners; earnings for financial planners that are received entirely from fees from consultation, plan development, or investment management; these fees may be charged on an hourly or project basis depending on clients' needs or on a percentage of assets under management

liabilities debts or money owed

mutual funds a group of financial assets (such as stocks)

net income profit after taxes

net worth value found by subtracting all liabilities from all assets

stock a representation of financial ownership in a company; the value of a stock can rise or fall based on a company's performance or other factors

Financial planners who work with people who are very rich are called *private bankers* or *wealth managers*. They usually have a more hands-on role in managing and investing their clients' money. They work closely with accountants, financial analysts, lawyers, and other professionals.

Financial planners must also know about asset management, employee benefits, insurance, and investments. They must have good people skills, since it is important to have good relationships with clients. They must be able to explain complicated financial terms and programs in a way that regular people can understand.

Financial planners use various ways to find new clients, such as telephone calls, emails, and giving seminars on financial planning.

Education and Training

In high school, you should take as many business classes as possible, as well as math. Courses in communications, speech, or acting will help put you at ease with talking in front of a crowd. English classes will help you prepare written reports.

Most financial planners earn a bachelor's degree in business, finance, accounting, economics, mathematics, or law. Others earn a business administration degree with a specialty in financial planning. Still others earn a liberal arts degree with courses in accounting, business administration, economics, finance, marketing, human behavior, counseling, and public speaking.

Earnings

The U.S. Department of Labor reports that financial planners earned median annual salaries of $69,050 in 2008. The most experienced financial planners with the highest level of education earned more than $119,000. The least experienced financial planners earned less than $34,000.

Outlook

Employment of financial planners is expected to grow rapidly in the future. When the economy is good, people earn more

FOR MORE INFO

For information on financial planning and certification, contact

Certified Financial Planner Board of Standards
1425 K Street, NW, Suite 500
Washington, DC 20005-3686
800-487-1497
mail@CFPBoard.org
http://www.cfp.net

For information on financial planning, visit the association's Web site.

Financial Planning Association
4100 East Mississippi Avenue, Suite 400
Denver, CO 80246-3053
800-322-4237
http://www.fpanet.org

This organization represents the professional interests of fee-only financial advisers. Visit its Web site for answers to frequently asked questions about the field.

National Association of Personal Financial Advisors
3250 North Arlington Heights Road, Suite 109
Arlington Heights, IL 60004-1574
847-483-5400
info@napfa.org
http://www.napfa.org

and inherit more. This means they will have more money to invest. More and more people will need advice from financial planners on how to invest their money. Competition for these jobs is strong. Many people want to become financial planners. Planners with certification, a college degree, and experience in sales will have the best job prospects.

Geophysicists

What Geophysicists Do

Geophysics is an important field that combines the sciences of geology and physics. Geology is the study of the history and composition of the Earth as recorded by rock formations and fossils. Physics deals with all forms of energy, the properties of matter, and the relationship between energy and matter.

Geophysicists study the physical structure of the Earth. This includes land surfaces, underground areas, and bodies of water, such as oceans, lakes, and rivers. They use their knowledge to predict earthquakes, discover oil, and find safe places to build power plants. Their duties may include fieldwork, laboratory research, or college teaching.

Geophysicists often study environmental issues. For example, they may investigate whether an explosion designed to expose rich mineral deposits might also lead to an earthquake. They might examine the quality of underground water and how it affects a city's drinking supply.

EXPLORING

- You can find out more about geophysics by reading books on rocks and minerals, metals and metallurgy (the study of the physical and chemical properties of metals), the universe and space, and weather and climate. Here is one suggestion: *Planet Earth: What Planet Are You On?*, by Dan Green (Kingfisher, 2010).
- Develop hobbies that deal with radio, electronics, rock collecting, or map collecting.
- Visit the Society of Exploration Geophysicists kids' Web site, http://students.seg.org/kids.
- Talk to a geophysicist about his or her career.

A volcanologist studies a solid lava sample following the eruption of Mt. Etna, one of Europe's largest active volcanoes. (Fabrizio Villa, AP Photo)

Geophysicists usually specialize in one area of geophysics. For example, *seismologists* study earthquakes. They use seismographs and other instruments to record the location of earthquakes and the vibrations they cause. They examine active fault lines and areas where earthquakes have occurred. *Hydrologists* study the movement and distribution of surface and underground waters. The information that they collect is applied to problems in flood control, crop production, soil and water conservation, irrigation, and inland water projects. Some hydrologists study glaciers.

DID YOU KNOW?

- Scientists believe that the San Andreas fault may be 100 million years old. It cuts through the state of California for almost 700 miles. Small earthquakes along the San Andreas fault occur several times a month. Not all earthquakes are dangerous, but many lives have been lost due to earthquakes along the fault. In the 1906 San Francisco earthquake, 500 people died from falling buildings and fires. The city burned for three days.

- There are more than a million quakes around the world each year, including those too small to be felt.

- An earthquake occurs once every 30 seconds.

- The most people killed in an earthquake is approximately 830,000 in China in 1556.

- The great Alaska earthquake of March 27, 1964, was the strongest earthquake in the United States. It had a magnitude of 9.2. Approximately 122 people died, with most of the deaths due to the tsunami (a seismic ocean wave) it generated. Shaking was felt for an estimated seven minutes, and raised or lowered the ground surface as much as 56 feet in some areas.

- A magnitude 9.5 earthquake in Chile in 1960 was the largest known earthquake and resulted in more than 6,000 deaths. It triggered a tsunami that killed people as far away as Hawaii and Japan.

- Alaska has more earthquakes per year than the combined total of the rest of the United States. As many as 4,000 are recorded there every year.

Source: Center for Earthquake Research and Information, University of Memphis

Geodesists measure the shape and size of the Earth to determine fixed points, positions, and elevations on or near the Earth's surface. *Geomagnetists* use specialized equipment to measure variations in the Earth's magnetic field from magnetic observatories and stations. *Applied geophysicists* use data gathered from the air and ground, as well as computers, to analyze the Earth's crust. They look for oil and mineral deposits and try to find places that can be used to safely dispose of hazardous wastes. *Exploration geophysicists,* sometimes called *geophysical prospectors,* use seismic techniques to look for possible oil and gas deposits. *Volcanologists* study volcanoes, their location, and their activity. *Planetologists* study the makeup and atmosphere of the planets, the Moon, and other bodies in our solar system.

No matter what their area of specialization, geophysicists use the scientific principles of geology, chemistry, mathematics, physics, and engineering. Many of their instruments, such as the seismograph, take precise measurements of the earth's

Helping Hands: Geoscientists Without Borders

You may be familiar with the organization Doctors Without Borders, a group of physicians and other health care workers who travel the world to volunteer their time to help people affected by poverty, war, and natural disasters.

But did you know that there is now a similar organization for geoscientists? Geoscientists Without Borders, which is sponsored by the Society of Exploration Geophysicists (SEG), "applies geophysical technology to the needs of people from all areas of the globe through targeted projects designed to tangibly impact the community around them." The SEG Foundation provides grants to colleges and universities that then send geoscience students and professionals around the world to conduct humanitarian and community geoscience projects.

Clemson University, one of the first grant recipients, partnered with the Foundation for Economic Security (a nongovernmental organization in India) and the Indian Institute of Technology to help villagers in Madhya Pradesh, India, affected by drought and poor quality water. Participants searched for ways to capture water runoff from precipitation and increase supplies of groundwater during the dry season, developed irrigation plans for farming to put less stress on groundwater supplies, and used their training to search for new sources of groundwater. Visit http://www.seg.org/gwb for more information about Geoscientists Without Borders and its current projects.

Tips for Success

To be a successful geophysicist, you should

- be very good at math and science
- have an interest in conducting experiments
- like solving problems
- enjoy working outdoors
- be able to work well as a member of a team
- be willing to continue to learn throughout your career

physical characteristics, such as its electric, magnetic, and gravitational fields. *Field geophysicists* work outdoors in all kinds of weather. They often travel and work in remote areas. They may be away from home for long periods of time.

Education and Training

Geophysicists should have a solid background in math and the physical and earth sciences. In high school you should take four years of math and courses in earth science, physics, and chemistry. Classes in mechanical drawing, history, and English are also highly recommended.

The best way to become a geophysicist is to get a bachelor's degree in geophysics, geoscience, or geology. A degree in physics, mathematics, or chemistry might be sufficient, but you should also take as many geology courses as you can. You will need a master's degree or doctorate in geophysics, geoscience, or geology for research or college teaching positions and other positions with good advancement potential. Learning a foreign language will be helpful if you plan to work overseas.

Earnings

According to the U.S. Department of Labor, geoscientists (a career category that includes geophysicists, geologists, and other related workers) earned an average annual salary of $79,160 in 2008. Salaries ranged from less than $41,000 to more than $155,000 annually. In 2008, the average salary for a geophysicist working for the federal government was $91,030.

FOR MORE INFO

For information on geoscience careers, contact
American Geological Institute
4220 King Street
Alexandria, VA 22302-1502
703-379-2480
http://www.agiweb.org

For industry information, contact
American Geophysical Union
2000 Florida Avenue, NW
Washington, DC 20009-1277
800-966-2481
http://www.agu.org

For career information and profiles of women in geophysics, visit the association's Web site.
Association for Women Geoscientists
1400 West 122nd Avenue, Suite 250
Westminster, CO 80234-3499
303-412-6219
office@awg.org
http://www.awg.org

For career information, contact
Seismological Society of America
201 Plaza Professional Building
El Cerrito, CA 94530
510-525-5474
info@seismosoc.org
http://www.seismosoc.org

For information on careers in geophysics, contact
Society of Exploration Geophysicists
PO Box 702740
Tulsa, OK 74170-2740
918-497-5500
http://www.seg.org

For information on the geosciences and to read the online publication *Become a Geophysicist . . . A What?*, visit the following Web sites:
U.S. Geological Survey
http://www.usgs.gov/education
http://earthquake.usgs.gov/learn/kids/become.php

Outlook

Many geophysicists explore for oil and gas. Their employment opportunities depend on the strength of the petroleum industry. But even if job prospects in the oil industry are not good, there will continue to be jobs in teaching and other research areas. There is also demand for geophysicists to work in land and resource protection. Geophysicists who speak a foreign language and who are willing to work abroad will have the best job prospects.

Math Teachers

What Math Teachers Do

Math teachers help students learn simple and advanced math theories and apply these concepts to everyday life. They work in elementary, middle, and high school classrooms. Some math teachers may also work as adult education teachers. Professors are teachers who work at the college level.

Math teachers teach complex mathematical subjects such as algebra, calculus, geometry, trigonometry, and statistics to middle and high school students. They may teach algebra to a class of ninth graders one period and trigonometry to high school seniors the next. Teachers must be able to get along with young people, have patience, and like to help others. They need good communication skills, since they often work with students from varying ethnic backgrounds and cultures.

Math teachers not only teach specific subjects, but they must make learning fun and teach students how to work together. Some schools use less structured classrooms to teach math skills, team problem solving, and cooperation. Math teachers encourage creative and logical thinking as it relates to math and education in general. They often use various teaching methods to keep students interested and help them learn. They may use games, computers, and experiments as hands-on teaching tools in the classroom. They may schedule field trips, guest speakers, or special events to show students how math skills are used in their daily lives and in the operation of businesses and government.

EXPLORING

- Visit the Web sites of professional associations to learn more about careers in math. The American Mathematical Society's Web site, http://www.ams.org, offers information on math careers, competitions, and publications. Additionally, the National Council of Teachers of Mathematics offers information on becoming a math teacher at its Web site, http://www.nctm.org/resources/content.aspx?id=530.
- By attending your own math classes, you've already gained a good sense of the daily work of a math teacher. But teachers have many duties beyond the classroom, so ask to spend some time with one of your teachers after school. Ask about his or her job, how he or she prepared for the career, and look at lecture notes and record-keeping procedures.
- Teach your younger sister or brother to count or do basic arithmetic, such as addition and subtraction. As they get a little older, you can teach them the value of coins and how to make change.
- Your school or community may have a volunteer program where you can tutor younger children in math.

Math teachers also develop lesson plans, create exams, correct papers, calculate grades, and keep records. Some schools may also require teachers to lead extracurricular activities such as math club, competitions, and events. Teachers meet with and advise students, hold parent/teacher conferences, and attend faculty meetings. In addition, they may have to attend local, state, and national conferences. Teachers must take continuing education courses to maintain their state's teaching license.

A math teacher discusses a lesson with a student. (Bob Daemmrich, The Image Works)

Words to Learn

algebra the mathematical study of numerical relationships between things that change over time

calculus a system used to analyze rates of change in mathematical quantities that are related to one another

geometry literally means measuring the Earth; this branch of math deals with measuring the elements of three-dimensional space, like points, lines, and angles

probability the likelihood that something will happen; mathematical computations are used to determine probability

statistics a mathematical science that organizes many facts into a systematized picture of data

trigonometry a mathematical method to find the unknown measurements of a geometric shape such as a triangle

Education and Training

If you want to pursue a career as a math teacher, you should take high school math courses including algebra, geometry, trigonometry, and calculus. More advanced classes such as probability, statistics, and logic are also beneficial if they are available. Computer science, psychology, and English classes are also recommended.

There are more than 500 accredited teacher education programs in the United States. Most of these programs are designed to meet the certification requirements for the state in which they are located. Some states may require that you pass a test before being admitted to an education program. You may choose to major in mathematics while taking required education courses, or you may major in secondary education with

DID YOU KNOW?

We use math every day in all kinds of ways. Here are some examples:

- **Art**. Artists use triangles, squares, rectangles, circles, and other geometric shapes. Some artists use math when they create special formulas to mix their own paints, chemicals, or other materials.
- **Health**. Temperature, heart rate, pulse, and blood pressure all are measured in numbers. Diet and nutrition use basic math to figure calories, fat grams, and recommended daily allowances. Doctors use math to figure dosages for drugs.
- **Music**. Rhythm is based on counting. Think of whole notes, half notes, quarter notes, and eighth notes and you are thinking in fractions.
- **Sports**. Math is used in sports for scoring, figuring averages and percentages, and compiling statistics.

a concentration in math. Although requirements for teaching licenses vary by state, all public schools require teachers to have a bachelor's degree and complete the state's approved training program.

Earnings

According to the U.S. Department of Labor, the median annual salary for secondary school teachers was $51,180 in 2008. Salaries ranged from less than $34,000 to $81,000 or more annually. The median annual salary of middle school teachers was $49,700 in 2008. Those just starting out in the field earned less than $34,000. Very experienced teachers earned more than $78,000. College math professors earned an average salary of $61,120 a year in 2008.

Outlook

Teachers are generally in short supply across the nation due to rising school enrollments and the number of teachers who are

FOR MORE INFO

For more information on a teaching career, contact

American Federation of Teachers
555 New Jersey Avenue, NW
Washington, DC 20001-2029
202-879-4400
online@aft.org
http://www.aft.org

For information on careers in mathematics, contact

American Mathematical Society
201 Charles Street
Providence, RI 02904-2213
800-321-4AMS
ams@ams.org
http://www.ams.org

For information on opportunities for women in the mathematical sciences and profiles of female mathematicians, contact

Association for Women in Mathematics
11240 Waples Mill Road, Suite 200
Fairfax, VA 22030-6078
703-934-0163
awm@awm-math.org
http://www.awm-math.org

For information on competitions for high school students, contact

Mathematical Association of America
1529 Eighteenth Street, NW
Washington, DC 20036-1358
800-741-9415
maahq@maa.org
http://www.maa.org

For information on teaching careers in mathematics, contact

National Council of Teachers of Mathematics
1906 Association Drive
Reston, VA 20191-1502
800-235-7566
nctm@nctm.org
http://www.nctm.org

For information on public education, contact

National Education Association
1201 16th Street, NW
Washington, DC 20036-3290
202-833-4000
http://www.nea.org

retiring. Math teachers are especially needed. According to surveys conducted by the American Federation of Teachers, school districts report a considerable shortage of math teachers, with greater shortages occurring in large cities.

Operations Research Analysts

What Operations Research Analysts Do

Operations research analysts are problem solvers. They help companies work more smoothly and with less waste of time and money. They may, for example, help design the layout of a grocery store or choose the best location for one. Or they may figure out how an insurance company can introduce new customer services with the least cost and confusion.

The job duties of analysts vary depending on their employers, but all follow the same general steps in doing their work. First, company managers describe a business problem to the analyst. For example, a bank president might want to improve ways to process checks. He or she also might want to know which workers should be involved in each part of the system. The analyst then makes a mathematical model of how checks are currently processed. To do this, he or she divides the present system into

EXPLORING

- Visit http://www.scienceofbet ter.org to learn more about operations research.
- Ask your math teacher to set up a talk with an operations research analyst to help you learn more about the field.
- Because this field requires advanced study, it is hard to get hands-on experience while in school. However, if you are in high school, you can try to get a part-time job with a bank or insurance company that has an in-house operations research department. This will give you some exposure to the career.
- Consider enrolling in special summer sessions or advanced placement mathematics courses to further develop your knowledge of mathematics.

steps, giving a number value to each step. Then the analyst studies the mathematical relationships between the steps. The model can be changed to figure out what will happen to the system under different conditions. Many models are computerized. Thus, analysts need to be able to use or write computer programs.

Analysts may take several weeks or months to solve a problem. They research the current system, evaluate it, and redesign it. Larger organizations may have systems that involve hundreds of employees in dozens of different departments.

Tips for Success

To be a successful operations research analyst, you should

- be very good at math
- be able to use computers
- be attentive to detail
- have the ability to work well with others
- be energetic
- have good communication skills
- like to solve problems

Operations research analysts work for a variety of employers. These include manufacturers of machinery and transportation equipment, computer systems design firms, banks, telecommunications companies, insurance companies, scientific and technical consulting services firms, and management consultants. The federal government, especially the U.S. Department of Defense, also hires analysts. State and local government agencies also employ operations research analysts. Operations research analysts often work as part of a research team consisting of other mathematicians and engineers, and they frequently use data-processing equipment in their research. They prepare written and oral reports of their findings for upper-level management.

Education and Training

School courses that can help you prepare for this career include math, economics, English composition, and computer science.

DID YOU KNOW?

- Operations research was developed during World War II to help determine the best way to send supplies, organize troops, and set up radar to find enemy submarines. It helped military planners manage massive amounts of supplies and millions of troops.
- More than 130 colleges and universities offer programs or courses in operations research, management science, decision sciences, and related fields.
- The Institute for Operations Research and the Management Sciences has about 13,000 members. About 56 percent of its members are employed at colleges and universities, 35 percent in private industry, and 9 percent in government and military positions.

Source: Institute for Operations Research and the Management Sciences

According to the Institute for Operations Research and the Management Sciences, math classes that are especially important include linear algebra, statistics, probability, calculus, and other advanced math classes.

Some employers want analysts to have a bachelor's degree in mathematics, business administration (management), operations research, or management science. Others expect employees to have master's degrees in one of these fields. More employers are looking for analysts with degrees in computer science, information systems, engineering, business, applied mathematics, or information systems. Analysts who work for the government usually have to pass a civil service examination. New employees usually get several months of on-the-job training. Those with little or no experience work closely with experienced analysts during this period.

Earnings

The median annual salary of operations research analysts was $69,000 in 2008, according to the U.S. Department of Labor. Salaries ranged from less than $40,000 to $118,000 or more each year. Operations research analysts who work for the federal government usually earn higher salaries than those in private companies.

FOR MORE INFO

For more information about a career as an operations research analyst, contact
American Mathematical Society
201 Charles Street
Providence, RI 02904-2213
800-321-4AMS
ams@ams.org
http://www.ams.org

For information on opportunities for women in the mathematical sciences and profiles of female mathematicians, contact
Association for Women in Mathematics
11240 Waples Mill Road, Suite 200
Fairfax, VA 22030-6078
703-934-0163
awm@awm-math.org
http://www.awm-math.org

For information on careers and educational programs, contact
Institute for Operations Research and the Management Sciences

7240 Parkway Drive, Suite 300
Hanover, MD 21076-1310
800-446-3676
informs@informs.org
http://www.informs.org

For information on competitions for high school students, contact
Mathematical Association of America
1529 Eighteenth Street, NW
Washington, DC 20036-1358
800-741-9415
maahq@maa.org
http://www.maa.org

For information on careers, contact
Society for Industrial and Applied Mathematics
3600 University City Science Center
Philadelphia, PA 19104-2688
215-382-9800
http://www.siam.org

Outlook

There will be excellent employment opportunities in operations research in the next decade. Analysts will be in demand to help companies increase their productivity or lower operating costs. There will be many opportunities for those with graduate degrees in operations research or management science.

Optical Engineers

What Optical Engineers Do

Optics is the study of light and how it interacts with matter. It is a branch of physics and engineering. *Optical engineers* use their knowledge of how light is produced, sent, detected, and measured to design such things as wireless communications, CD/DVD players, high-definition television, and computer-related products such as wireless mice and laser printers. It is also used in atomic research, defense technology intended to stop terrorist attacks, robotics, and medical and scientific methods and tools.

Optical engineers may design optical systems for digital cameras, telescopes, or lens systems. They fine-tune optical devices. They design and develop circuitry and parts for devices that use optical technology. These engineers may also design and test instruments that measure how well optical systems are working.

To create a new product using optical technology, optical engineers follow a process that has many steps. They study the problem to understand it thoroughly. Then they use their imagination and training to come up with a solution for the problem. Once they have an idea, they turn it into a design or several designs. They use computer software to create a model, or they make a sample. They test the model or sample and change it as they find problems. They repeat this building and testing until they feel that their work is complete. The design is then sent to a company that manufactures the product. Optical engineers often work as part of a team of engineers, industrial designers, technologists, and technicians.

EXPLORING

- SPIE, an international society for optics and photonics, offers the following videos that will help you learn more about the field: *Light in Action: Lasers, Cameras & Other Cool Stuff; Optics: Light at Work;* and *Careers in Optics.* Visit http://spie.org/x30120.xml to view them online or order free DVDs.
- Visit the following Web site to learn more about optics: Exploring the Science of Light! (http://www.opticsforteens.org).
- Visit http://www.opticsforteens.org/terms/general.html for an optics glossary.
- Your teacher or librarian can help you find books and magazines on optics.
- Join science and engineering clubs that offer opportunities for experimentation, problem-solving, and team-building activities.
- Ask your teacher or a parent to help you perform simple experiments that examine the properties of light. Books on optics often provide instructions for experiments.
- Talk to an optical engineer about his or her career.

Some optical engineers specialize in lasers and fiber optics. They are known as *fiber optics engineers* and *laser and fiber optics engineers.* Fiber optics are thin, hairlike strands of plastic-coated glass fibers that transmit light and images. Lasers may be used to generate the light in these fibers. Lasers are devices that produce thin, powerful beams of light. They can be used in medical and surgical procedures, manufacturing, robotics, printing, and military systems, such as navigation systems and weapons systems. Fiber optics technology is used in sensors that detect temperature, pressure, and other physical features. This technology is also used in communications systems such as telephone systems, computer networks, and fiber optic imaging, which

DID YOU KNOW?

Where Optical Engineers Work

- Laboratories
- Hospitals
- Colleges and universities
- Computer industry
- Telecommunications industry
- Construction industry
- Government agencies
- Any company or organization that uses optical technology

Options for Optical Engineers

Optics is a growing field. Optical engineers today work in these areas:

- Information processing
- Wireless communications
- CD/DVD technology
- High-definition television
- Laser printers
- Astronomical observation
- Atomic research
- Robotics
- Military surveillance
- Water-quality monitoring
- Undersea monitoring
- Medical and scientific procedures and instruments

involves the use of fiber optics to transmit light or images.

Education and Training

In high school, take physical science, physics, chemistry, geometry, algebra, trigonometry, calculus, social studies, English, composition, and computer science classes. Courses in computer-aided design will also be helpful.

You must have a bachelor of science degree in engineering to become an optical engineer. Many colleges offer classes in optics. Only a very small number of schools, though, offer degree programs in optical engineering. Most colleges offer degrees in a related field, such as electrical engineering or physics, with a specialization in optics. Most programs take four or five years to complete. Some colleges require internships or cooperative work programs during which you work at a related job for one to three semesters.

Many students receive master's degrees in optical engineering or a related field. Those who plan to work in research usually earn a doctoral degree.

Earnings

Entry-level optical engineers earned a median annual salary

FOR MORE INFO

For information on engineering careers and student clubs and competitions, contact

Junior Engineering Technical Society
1420 King Street, Suite 405
Alexandria, VA 22314-2750
703-548-5387
info@jets.org
http://www.jets.org

For information on careers, contact the following organizations:

IEEE Photonics Society
c/o The Institute of Electrical and Electronics Engineers
445 Hoes Lane
Piscataway, NJ 08854-4141
http://www.ieee.org/portal/site/leos

Optical Society of America
2010 Massachusetts Avenue, NW
Washington, DC 20036-1023
202-223-8130
info@osa.org
http://www.osa.org

For information on science fairs and to view videos about optics, visit the SPIE Web site.

SPIE
PO Box 10
Bellingham, WA 98227-0010
888-504-8171
customerservice@spie.org
http://www.spie.org

of $88,570 a year in 2008, according to the U.S. Department of Labor. Those engineers just starting out in the field earned less than $49,000. The highest paid optical engineers earned more than $132,000.

Outlook

Opportunities for optical engineers will be very good in the next decade. New uses for optics technology are discovered all the time. The use of fiber optics technology in telecommunications is increasing. This means that there will be more opportunities for engineers in the computer, broadcasting, cable, and telecommunications industries. Optical engineers will also find jobs in the medical and defense fields.

Physicists

What Physicists Do

Physicists try to understand the laws of nature and learn how to use these laws in ways that will help people in their daily lives. Some teach in high schools and colleges, some work for the federal government, and some work for industrial laboratories. Wherever they work, physicists spend a great deal of time doing research, conducting experiments, and studying the results.

Physicists are concerned with the special properties of matter (solids, liquids, and gases) and energy. *Theoretical physicists* try to understand how matter and energy work. For example, they may study electrical or nuclear energy, try to define the laws of each, and then write up their findings in mathematical formulas. *Experimental physicists* perform experiments that test exactly what various kinds of matter and energy do. Then they try to come up with practical ways to use them. For example, they may work in the communications industries, such as television, telephone, radio, or Internet, to invent technologies for better pictures or better sound.

Physicists work in many areas. Physicists may specialize in mechanics, heat, optics (light), acoustics (sound), electricity and magnetism, electronics, particle physics (atoms and molecules), nuclear physics, or physics of fluids. Others work with engineers to find the best ways to build bridges and dams. Others conduct experiments for petroleum companies to find better ways to obtain, refine, and use crude oil. Physicists are important to the space program. Known as *astrophysicists*, they try to

EXPLORING

- Read books about physics. Here are some suggestions: *Physics: Why Matter Matters!*, by Dan Green (Kingfisher, 2008); *The Manga Guide to Physics,* by Hideo Nitta and Keita Takatsu (No Starch Press, 2009); *Flying Circus of Physics,* 2nd edition, by Jearl Walker (Wiley, 2006); and *George's Secret Key to the Universe* and *George's Cosmic Treasure Hunt,* both by Stephen and Lucy Hawking (Simon & Schuster Children's Publishing, 2009).
- Visit the American Physical Society's Web site for students, http://www.aps.org/careers/student. It features information on recommended middle and high school classes, interviews with physics professionals, and an overview of career opportunities. Another excellent site is PhysicsCentral (http://www.physicscentral.com).
- Ask your science teachers to assign some physics experiments.
- Join a science club or start one at your school.
- Enter a project in a science fair. If your school does not sponsor science fairs, you may find fairs sponsored by your school district, state, or a science society.
- Talk to a physicist about his or her career. Ask your science teacher or counselor to help you set up an interview.

figure out what outer space is actually like, and they design and test spaceships.

Although biology and geology are separate sciences in their own right, the concepts of physics can also be applied directly to them. Where this application has been made, a new series of sciences has developed. To separate them from their parent sciences, they are known by such names as biophysics (the physics of living things) and geophysics (the physics of the Earth).

A physicist (right) *and a company executive examine a bench-scale prototype of a decontamination filtration system the company is developing.* (Mike Derer, AP Photo)

Similarly, the sciences of chemistry and physics sometimes overlap in subject matter as well as in viewpoint and procedure, creating physical chemistry.

All physicists must have keen powers of observation, have a strong curiosity about the world around them, and enjoy solving problems. They are detail oriented, precise, and good communicators. Physicists should have patience and be able to work alone or on research teams. They should also be willing to continue to learn throughout their careers.

Education and Training

In high school, take as much mathematics (algebra, advanced algebra, and calculus) as is offered, and explore as many of the sciences as possible. English skills are important, as physicists must write up their results, communicate with other scientists, and lecture on their findings. In addition, get as much experience as possible using computers.

There are some jobs available for physicists who have only a bachelor's degree from a four-year college. If you have a bachelor's degree, you may be able to find a basic research job. If you have a teaching certificate, you can teach at a high school.

Most physicists will need to go on for further education if they want to advance in the field. The more challenging and rewarding jobs go to physicists who have master's degrees and doctorates. Many of the most able physicists go on to complete postdoctoral education.

DID YOU KNOW?

Where Physicists Work

- Federal government (U.S. Departments of Defense, Energy, Health and Human Services, and Commerce, national laboratories, and for the National Aeronautics and Space Administration)
- State government
- Private companies
- Colleges and universities
- Hospitals

Earnings

The median salary for physicists was $102,890 in 2008, according to the U.S. Department of Labor. Salaries ranged from less than $57,000 to $159,000 or more. Physicists employed by the federal government had mean annual earnings of $108,020. The most highly paid physicists have doctoral degrees and many years of experience.

Fame & Fortune: Stephen Hawking (1942–   )

Stephen Hawking is an English theoretical astrophysicist. He has conducted groundbreaking work on black holes, general relativity, cosmology, space-time singularities, and other research topics. But Hawking is best known for his books and public appearances that have explained astrophysics to everyday people. His books include *A Brief History of Time, Black Holes and Baby Universes and Other Essays, The Universe in a Nutshell,* and *A Briefer History of Time.* He has appeared on popular television shows such as *Star Trek: The Next Generation, The Simpsons,* and *Futurama. A Brief History of Time,* a film about Hawking's life, was released in 1991.

Hawking's story is especially inspiring because he has dedicated his life to scientific investigation despite being severely disabled. In college, Hawking was diagnosed with amyotrophic lateral sclerosis. The condition gradually causes loss of mobility (paralysis) in the limbs—and eventually death. Hawking uses a wheelchair and can no longer speak as a result of a lung infection he contracted in 1985. He now uses a voice synthesizer to communicate. Despite these challenges, Hawking has become one of the most respected and well-known physicists in the world. He held the post of Lucasian Professor of Mathematics at Cambridge University for 30 years. Hawking refuses to let his disability stop him from studying the universe.

In recent years, Hawking published two children's books—*George's Secret Key to the Universe* and *George's Cosmic Treasure Hunt*—with his daughter Lucy. The adventure-oriented books explain the universe. In 2009, Hawking was awarded the Presidential Medal of Freedom, the highest civilian award in the United States. Hawking continues to conduct research into theoretical physics and give public lectures about the field.

Visit http://www.hawking.org.uk to learn more about Stephen Hawking and his work.

Sources: Hawking.org.uk

Famous Physics Labs

These are some of the Department of Energy's research and development facilities:

- Brookhaven National Laboratory (http://www.bnl.gov/world) in Upton, Long Island, New York, is mainly involved in studies of nuclear physics. It also does chemical, biological, environmental, medical imaging, neuroscience, and nonproliferation research.
- Fermi National Accelerator Laboratory (http://www.fnal.gov) in Batavia, Illinois, conducts research in high-energy physics.
- Lawrence Berkeley National Laboratory (http://www.lbl.gov) in Berkeley, California, conducts research in fundamental studies of the universe, quantitative biology, nanoscience, new energy systems and environmental solutions, and integrated computing.
- Los Alamos National Laboratory (http://www.lanl.gov) in Los Alamos, New Mexico, conducts research in nuclear weapons and energy, cryogenic physics, space sciences, molecular biology, and metallurgy.

Outlook

Employment for physicists should be good during the next decade. Increases in government research, particularly in the Departments of Defense and Energy, will create more opportunities for physicists. Physics-related research in the private sector is expected to decline. The U.S. Department of Labor predicts that there will be many opportunities for graduate-level physicists outside of traditional physics fields. They will have job titles such as computer programmer, computer

FOR MORE INFO

For employment statistics and information on jobs and career planning, contact
American Institute of Physics
One Physics Ellipse
College Park, MD 20740-3843
301-209-3100
aipinfo@aip.org
http://www.aip.org

For information on educational requirements and careers, contact
American Physical Society
One Physics Ellipse
College Park, MD 20740-3844
301-209-3200
http://www.aps.org

Fermilab is a U.S. Department of Energy research and development laboratory. Visit the following Web sites to learn more about the laboratory and precollege education programs:
Fermi National Accelerator Laboratory
Education Office
Fermilab MS 226
Box 500
Batavia, IL 60510-5011
630-840-3092
http://www.fnal.gov
http://www.fnal.gov/pub/education/k-12
_programs.html

software engineer, or systems analyst or developer, rather than physicist. Those with just a bachelor's degree in physics will find opportunities as high school physics teachers and in occupational areas such as mathematics, computer science, engineering, environmental science, and finance.

Software Designers

What Software Designers Do

Without software, computers would not be able to work. The term *software* was coined to differentiate it from "hardware," which refers to the physical parts of the computer system. Software is the set of mathematical codes that tells a computer what to do. A set of instructions that directs a computer's hardware to perform a task is called a software program. There are three types of software. *System software* controls a computer's internal functioning, usually through an operating system, and runs such extras as monitors, printers, and storage devices. *Application software* directs the computer to carry out commands given by the user. Application software includes word processing, spreadsheet, database management, inventory, and payroll programs. *Network software* coordinates communication between the computers that are linked in a network.

Software designers create software programs, also called applications. *Computer programmers* then create the software by writing the code that gives the computer instructions.

Software designers must imagine every detail of what a software application will do, how it will do it, and how it will look on the screen. An example is how a home accounting program is created. The software designer first decides what the program should be able to do, such as balance a checkbook, keep track of incoming and outgoing bills, and keep records of expenses. For each of these tasks, the software designer decides what menus and icons to use, what each screen will look like, and whether there will be help or dialog boxes to assist the user. For example,

EXPLORING

- Read books about computers and careers in the field. Here are some suggestions: *Careers for Computer Buffs & Other Technological Types,* 3rd edition, by Marjorie Eberts (McGraw-Hill, 2006); *The Complete Idiot's Guide to Computer Basics,* 5th edition, by Joe Kraynak (Alpha, 2009); *Absolute Beginner's Guide to Computer Basics,* 5th edition, by Michael Miller (Que Publishing, 2009); and *How Computers Work,* 9th edition, by Ron White and Timothy Edward Downs (Que Publishing, 2007).
- Visit the Association for Computing Machinery's career Web site, http://computing-careers.acm.org, for information on career paths, a list of suggested high school classes, profiles of computer science students, and answers to frequently asked questions about the field.
- Learn as much as you can about computers. Take computer classes in school—especially those that focus on software design and computer programming.
- Keep up with new technology by reading computer magazines, visiting computer Web sites, and by talking to other computer users.
- Join computer clubs.
- Advanced students can put their design/programming knowledge to work by designing and programming their own applications, such as simple games and utility programs.
- Talk to a software designer about his or her career.

the designer may want the expense record part of the program to produce a pie chart that shows the percentage of each household expense in the overall household budget. The designer can ask that the program automatically display the pie chart each time a budget is completed or only after the user clicks on a special icon on the toolbar.

Microsoft Corp. Chairman Bill Gates, who began his career as a software designer, speaks to college students. (Andy Manis, AP Photo)

Tips for Success

To be a successful software designer, you should

- be detail oriented and have patience
- enjoy problem solving
- be able to work under deadline pressure
- have good communication skills
- be creative
- have excellent technical skills

Some software companies custom design software for the specific needs of one business. Some businesses are large enough that they employ in-house software designers who create software applications for their computer systems.

Software designers work throughout the United States, but opportunities are best in large cities and suburbs where business and industry are active. Programmers who develop software systems work for software manufacturers, many of whom are in California's Silicon Valley. There is also a concentration of software manufacturers in Boston, Chicago, and Atlanta, among other places. Designers who adapt and tailor the software to meet specific needs of end-users work for those end-user companies, many of which are scattered across the country.

Education and Training

Computer, science, and math classes will prepare you for a career as a software designer. In high school, you should take as many of these courses as possible. English and speech classes will help you improve your communication skills, which are important when making formal presentations to managers and clients once you enter the field.

To be a software designer, you will need at least a bachelor's degree in computer science plus at least one year of experience with a programming language. You also need knowledge of the field for which you will be designing software, such as education, entertainment, business, or science. For example, someone with a bachelor's degree in computer science with a minor in business or accounting has an excellent chance to land a job creating business and accounting software.

Earnings

The median salary for computer and information scientists (a job category that includes software designers) was $97,970 in 2008, according to the U.S. Department of Labor. Software designers just starting out in the field earned less than $57,000. Very experienced workers earned more than $151,000. At

Helping Hands: Bill and Melinda Gates

Bill Gates is the founder (along with Paul Allen) of the computer giant Microsoft. He is the richest person in the world. With all of the money he ever could need, Gates could have retired from Microsoft and lived a life of luxury. Instead, he wanted to do more and make a difference in the world.

In 1994, he created the William H. Gates Foundation, which focused on improving world health. In 1997, he and his wife Melinda (a computer professional whom he met at Microsoft) created the Gates Library Foundation, which sought to bring computers with Internet connections to libraries in the United States. This organization eventually refocused its mission to help low-income minority students prepare and pay for college. In 2000, the two organizations were merged to form the Bill & Melinda Gates Foundation. The foundation has awarded more than $21 billion in grants to organizations in the United States and more than 100 other countries throughout the world.

Bill and Melinda Gates travel the world advocating to end world poverty and support other causes. Visit http://www.gatesfoundation.org for more information about the foundation and Bill and Melinda Gates.

Source: Bill & Melinda Gates Foundation

FOR MORE INFO

For information on careers, contact
Association for Computing Machinery
2 Penn Plaza, Suite 701
New York, NY 10121-0701
800-342-6626
acmhelp@acm.org
http://www.acm.org

For information on career opportunities for women in computing, contact
Association for Women in Computing
41 Sutter Street, Suite 1006
San Francisco, CA 94104-4905
info@awc-hq.org
http://www.awc-hq.org

For information on computer careers and student programs, contact
IEEE Computer Society
1730 Massachusetts Avenue, NW
Washington, DC 20036-1992

202-371-0101
http://www.computer.org

For information on certification, contact
Institute for Certification of Computing Professionals
2350 East Devon Avenue, Suite 281
Des Plaines, IL 60018-4602
800-843-8227
office2@iccp.org
http://www.iccp.org

For industry information, contact
Software & Information Industry Association
1090 Vermont Avenue, NW, Sixth Floor
Washington, DC 20005-4095
202-289-7442
http://www.siia.net

the managerial level, salaries are even higher and can reach $175,000 or more.

Outlook

There will continue to be strong employment opportunities for software designers. Employment of software designers is expected to increase as technology advances. The expanding use of the Internet by businesses, as well as the growing use of software in cell phones and video games, has created great demand for skilled professionals to design software.

Software Engineers

What Software Engineers Do

Computers need to be told exactly what to do in order to function. Software is the set of mathematical codes that tells a computer what to do. A set of instructions that directs a computer's hardware to perform a task is called a program, or software program.

Businesses use computers to do complicated work for them. In many cases, their needs are so specialized that commercial software programs cannot perform the desired tasks. *Software engineers* change existing software or create new software to solve problems in many fields, including business, medicine, law, communications, aerospace, and science.

Software engineers fall into two basic categories. *Systems software engineers* build and maintain entire computer systems and networks for a company. *Applications software engineers* design, create, and modify general computer applications software or specialized utility programs.

The projects software engineers work on are all different, but their methods for solving a problem are similar. First, engineers talk to clients to find out their needs and to determine the problems they are having. Next, the engineers look at the software already used by the client to see if it can be changed or if entirely new software is needed. When they have all the facts, software engineers use scientific methods and mathematical models to figure out possible solutions to the problems. Then they choose the best solution and prepare a written proposal for managers and other engineers.

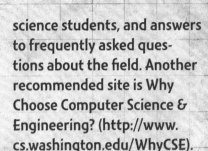

EXPLORING

- Read books about computers and careers in the field. Here are some suggestions: *Careers for Computer Buffs & Other Technological Types*, 3rd edition, by Marjorie Eberts (McGraw-Hill, 2006); *The Complete Idiot's Guide to Computer Basics*, 5th edition, by Joe Kraynak (Alpha, 2009); *Absolute Beginner's Guide to Computer Basics*, 5th edition, by Michael Miller (Que Publishing, 2009); and *How Computers Work*, 9th edition, by Ron White and Timothy Edward Downs (Que Publishing, 2007).
- Visit the Association for Computing Machinery's career Web site, http://computing-careers.acm.org, for information on career paths, a list of suggested high school classes, profiles of computer science students, and answers to frequently asked questions about the field. Another recommended site is Why Choose Computer Science & Engineering? (http://www.cs.washington.edu/WhyCSE).
- Learn as much as you can about computers, computer software, and computer hardware.
- Read computer magazines and talk to other computer users.
- Join computer clubs and search the Internet for information about working in this field.
- Try to spend a day with a working software engineer in order to experience the field firsthand. Your school counselor or teacher can help you arrange such a visit.

Once a proposal is accepted, software engineers and technicians check with hardware engineers to make sure computers are powerful enough to run the new programs. The software engineers then outline program details. *Computer software engineering technicians* write the initial version in computer languages.

Throughout the programming process, engineers and technicians run diagnostic tests on the program to make sure it is working well at every stage. They also meet regularly with the client to make sure they are meeting their goals and to learn about any changes the client wants.

When a software project is complete, the engineer prepares a demonstration of it for the client. Software engineers might also install the program, train users, and be ready to help with any problems that arise in the future.

DID YOU KNOW?

- The late John Tukey, professor of statistics at Princeton, coined the terms "software" and "bit."
- The first hard drive available for the Apple had a capacity of 5 megabytes. Today, the largest desktop hard drive has a storage capacity of 1.5 terabytes.
- The average mouse pad is eight and three quarters by seven and a half inches.

Software engineers work in a group office at Google Inc.'s campus in Kirkland, Washington. (Ted S. Warren, AP Photo)

To be a successful software engineer, you should have excellent technical skills and be willing to continue to learn throughout your career. You should be a good communicator in order to work as a member of a team and interact with people who have different levels of computer knowledge. You must also be detail oriented and work well under pressure.

Education and Training

Take as many computer, math, and science courses as possible in high school. English and speech courses will help you improve your communication skills, which are very important for software engineers.

At least a bachelor's degree is required to work as a software engineer. A typical degree concentration for an applications software engineer is software engineering, computer science, or mathematics. Systems software engineers typically pursue a concentration in computer science or computer information systems.

Earnings

Software engineers with a bachelor's degree in computer science received starting salaries of $61,407 in 2009, according to the National Association of Colleges and Employers. Salaries for software engineers ranged from less than $53,000 to more than $135,000 per year in 2008, according to the U.S. Department of Labor. Experienced software engineers earned more than $150,000 a year. Software engineers generally earn more in areas where there are lots of computer companies, such as California's Silicon Valley.

FOR MORE INFO

For information on careers, contact
Association for Computing Machinery
2 Penn Plaza, Suite 701
New York, NY 10121-0701
800-342-6626
acmhelp@acm.org
http://www.acm.org

For information on career opportunities for women in computing, contact
Association for Women in Computing
41 Sutter Street, Suite 1006
San Francisco, CA 94104-4905
info@awc-hq.org
http://www.awc-hq.org

For information on computer careers and student programs, contact
IEEE Computer Society
1730 Massachusetts Avenue, NW
Washington, DC 20036-1992

202-371-0101
http://www.computer.org

For information on certification, contact
Institute for Certification of Computing Professionals
2350 East Devon Avenue, Suite 281
Des Plaines, IL 60018-4602
800-843-8227
office2@iccp.org
http://www.iccp.org

For industry information, contact
Software & Information Industry Association
1090 Vermont Avenue, NW,
Sixth Floor
Washington, DC 20005-4095
202-289-7442
http://www.siia.net

Outlook

Employment for software engineers is expected to be excellent during the next decade. Computer networking, the growth of the Internet and communications technology that uses software, and increasing concern about cyber security are all fueling the need for software engineers. Those with bachelor's degrees and experience in the field will have the best job prospects. Computer companies, consulting firms, major corporations, insurance agencies, banks, and countless other industries hire software engineers.

Statisticians

What Statisticians Do

Statisticians use mathematics and statistical theory to collect and interpret information. Statisticians work in almost every kind of career field. Most statisticians work in one of three kinds of jobs: They may teach and research at a university, they may work in a governmental agency (such as the Census Bureau), or they may work in a business or industry. Some statisticians work for public opinion research companies. Their studies help us understand what different groups of people think about issues of the day.

Statisticians usually specialize in one of two areas. *Mathematical statisticians* think of new statistical methods and theories and create new ways to use these theories. *Applied statisticians* apply existing formulas to new questions. They may try to predict population growth or economic conditions, or estimate a crop yield (the amount of a crop—such as corn—that will be harvested each growing season).

EXPLORING

- Read books about math and statistics. Here is one suggestion: *The Manga Guide to Statistics*, by Shin Takahashi (No Starch Press, 2008).
- Ask your math teachers to show you a statistics textbook. They might be able to give you some simple statistical problems related to grades, for example.
- Ask your math teacher or counselor to arrange a visit to a local insurance agency, the local office of the Internal Revenue Service, or a nearby college to talk to people who use statistical methods.

DID YOU KNOW?

You probably know Florence Nightingale (1820–1910) as a famous nurse and pioneer in British health care reform. Did you know that she was also a statistician? When she was serving as a nurse during the Crimean War, she collected data using statistical techniques to find out how many British soldiers died because of unclean hospital conditions. She used this information to show why hospital conditions needed to be changed. By doing this, Nightingale showed how statistics can be used to improve medical and surgical practices.

In some cases, statisticians actually go out and gather the statistics they need. However, usually such facts are gathered by people who are trained especially in fact-gathering techniques. In the Census Bureau, for example, information is gathered by thousands of census takers. Once the census takers have gathered the information, it is given to statisticians. The statisticians then organize and analyze the information and make conclusions or recommendations about it.

Statisticians often have specialized job titles based on the type of field in which they are employed. *Econometricians* are statisticians who study economic data. *Biostatisticians*, also known as *biometricians, computational biologists,* and *bioinformatics specialists*, collect and analyze medical and public health data.

Education and Training

Statisticians must have strong mathematics and computer backgrounds. In

DID YOU KNOW?

Where Statisticians Work

- Federal government agencies (especially in the Departments of Commerce, Agriculture, and Health and Human Services)
- State and local government agencies
- Industry (especially in scientific research and development services, the insurance industry, and pharmaceutical and medicine manufacturing)
- Colleges and universities

What Sports Statisticians Do

Sports statisticians compute and record the statistics on a particular sports event, game, or competition. They use basic math and algebra and calculators and computers.

Most high school, college, and professional sports teams have an official *team scorer/statistician* who attends every home game and sits courtside, at what is called the scorer's table. The team scorer/statistician at a basketball game, for example, keeps track of the score, the number of time-outs, and specific calls made by the referees, such as team and player fouls. The statistician is also called the *official scorer* because if any item on the scoreboard is questioned—by a referee, one of the coaches, or another game official—the statistician is the one who provides the answer.

Some statisticians work by hand with a special notebook for recording the game statistics. As each play and call occurs in the game, the statistician writes down the play or call in a particular column or row of the stat book. Later, the statistician will add up the total number of player errors, rebounds, assists, or goals. He or she can use these numbers to figure out such statistics as the average number of rebounds in a quarter or in a game. Usually, the statistician keeps the stats for both the home team and the visiting team by individual. At the end of the game, the statistician can then provide both coaches and teams with specific information on their play during the game. Some statisticians use computers with specialized software programs that automatically compute the player and team statistics.

high school, you will need to take college preparatory classes in math, statistics, and computer science.

A bachelor's degree is the minimum requirement to get hired by the federal government. You will need a master's

FOR MORE INFO

For information on careers in mathematics, contact
American Mathematical Society
201 Charles Street
Providence, RI 02904-2213
800-321-4AMS
ams@ams.org
http://www.ams.org

For career information, contact
American Statistical Association
732 North Washington Street
Alexandria, VA 22314-1943
888-231-3473
asainfo@amstat.org
http://www.amstat.org

For information on opportunities for women in mathematics, contact
Association for Women in Mathematics
11240 Waples Mill Road, Suite 200
Fairfax, VA 22030-6078
703-934-0163
awm@awm-math.org
http://www.awm-math.org

For information on competitions for high school students, contact
Mathematical Association of America
1529 Eighteenth Street, NW
Washington, DC 20036-1358
800-741-9415
maahq@maa.org
http://www.maa.org

degree to work as a statistician for private companies. For some positions, though, you will need a doctoral degree. In college, many students choose a major in statistics or mathematics, or in the field they hope to work in, such as chemistry, computer science, or sociology.

Earnings

The U.S. Department of Labor reports that the median annual salary for statisticians was $72,610 in 2008. Salaries ranged from less than $39,000 to $117,000 or more annually. Statisticians employed by the federal government earned mean annual salaries of $92,332 in 2009.

Outlook

Good opportunities for statisticians are expected to continue during the next decade. Statisticians with advanced degrees or specialized training in computer science, engineering, biology, or finance should have good opportunities. Many of the current openings are in scientific and medical research.

Glossary

accredited approved as meeting established standards for providing good training and education; this approval is usually given by an independent organization of professionals

annual salary the money an individual earns for an entire year of work

apprentice a person who is learning a trade by working under the supervision of a skilled worker; apprentices often receive classroom instruction in addition to their supervised practical experience

associate's degree an academic rank or title granted by a community or junior college or similar institution to graduates of a two-year program of education beyond high school

bachelor's degree an academic rank or title given to a person who has completed a four-year program of study at a college or university; also called an **undergraduate degree** or **baccalaureate**

career an occupation for which a worker receives training and has an opportunity for advancement

certified approved as meeting established requirements for skill, knowledge, and experience in a particular field; people are certified by a professional organization in their field

college an educational institution that is above the high school level

community college a public or private two-year college attended by students who do not usually live at the college; graduates of a community college receive an associate's degree and may transfer to a four-year college or university to complete a bachelor's degree

diploma a certificate or document given by a school to show that a person has completed a course or has graduated from the school

distance education a type of educational program that allows students to take classes and complete their education by mail or the Internet

doctorate   the highest academic rank or title granted by a graduate school to a person who has completed a two- to three-year program after earning a master's degree

fellowship   a financial award given for research projects or dissertation assistance; fellowships are commonly offered at the graduate, postgraduate, or doctoral levels

freelancer   a worker who is not a regular employee of a company; freelancers work for themselves and do not receive a regular paycheck

fringe benefit   a payment or benefit to an employee in addition to regular wages or salary; examples of fringe benefits include a pension, a paid vacation, and health or life insurance

graduate school   a school that people may attend after they have received their bachelor's degree; people who complete an educational program at a graduate school earn a master's degree or a doctorate

intern   an advanced student (usually one with at least some college training) in a professional field who is employed in a job that is intended to provide supervised practical experience for the student

internship   1. the position or job of an intern; 2. the period of time when a person is an intern

junior college   a two-year college that offers courses like those in the first half of a four-year college program; graduates of a junior college usually receive an associate's degree and may transfer to a four-year college or university to complete a bachelor's degree

liberal arts   the subjects covered by college courses that develop broad general knowledge rather than specific occupational skills; the liberal arts are often considered to include philosophy, literature and languages, the arts, history, and some courses in the social sciences and natural sciences

major (in college)   the academic field in which a student specializes and receives a degree

master's degree   an academic rank or title granted by a graduate school to a person who has completed a one- or two-year program after earning a bachelor's degree

pension an amount of money paid regularly by an employer to a former employee after he or she retires from working

scholarship a gift of money to a student to help the student pay for further education

social studies courses of study (such as civics, geography, and history) that deal with how human societies work

starting salary salary paid to a newly hired employee; the starting salary is usually a smaller amount than is paid to a more experienced worker

technical college a private or public college offering two- or four-year programs in technical subjects; technical colleges offer courses in both general and technical subjects and award associate's degrees and bachelor's degrees

undergraduate a student at a college or university who has not yet received a degree

union an organization whose members are workers in a particular industry or company; the union works to gain better wages, benefits, and working conditions for its members; also called a **labor union** or **trade union**

vocational school a public or private school that offers training in one or more skills or trades

wage money that is paid in return for work done, especially money paid on the basis of the number of hours or days worked

Browse and Learn More

Books

Burnett, Rebecca. *Careers for Number Crunchers & Other Quantitative Types.* 2d ed. New York: McGraw-Hill, 2002.

Claverie, Jean-Michel, and Cedric Notredame. *Bioinformatics For Dummies.* 2d ed. Hoboken, N.J.: For Dummies, 2006.

Clemens, Meg, Glenn Clemens, and Sean Clemens. *The Everything Kids' Math Puzzles Book: Brain Teasers, Games, and Activities for Hours of Fun.* Cincinnati, Ohio: Adams Media Corporation, 2003.

Eberts, Marjorie. *Careers for Computer Buffs & Other Technological Types.* 3d ed. New York: McGraw-Hill, 2006.

Enzensberger, Hans Magnus. *The Number Devil: A Mathematical Adventure.* New York: Holt Paperbacks, 2000.

Fitzgerald, Theresa R. *Math Dictionary for Kids: The Essential Guide to Math Terms, Strategies, and Tables.* Waco, Tex.: Prufrock Press, 2005.

Gralla, Preston. *How the Internet Works.* 8th ed. Indianapolis: Que Publishing, 2006.

Green, Dan. *Astronomy: Out of This World!* New York: Kingfisher, 2009.

———. *Math: A Book You Can Count On.* New York: Kingfisher, 2010.

———. *Physics: Why Matter Matters!* New York: Kingfisher, 2008.

———. *Planet Earth: What Planet Are You On?* New York: Kingfisher, 2010.

Hawking, Stephen, and Lucy Hawking. *George's Cosmic Treasure Hunt.* New York: Simon & Schuster Children's Publishing, 2009.

———. *George's Secret Key to the Universe.* New York: Simon & Schuster Children's Publishing, 2009.

Kenji, Ishikawa. *The Manga Guide to the Universe.* San Francisco: No Starch Press, 2010.

Kojima, Hiroyuki. *The Manga Guide to Calculus.* San Francisco: No Starch Press, 2009.

Kraynak, Joe. *The Complete Idiot's Guide to Computer Basics.* 5th ed. New York: Alpha, 2009.

Lambert, Stephen. *Great Jobs for Math Majors.* 2d ed. New York: McGraw-Hill, 2005.

Long, Lynette. *Math Smarts: Tips, Tricks, and Secrets for Making Math More Fun!* Middleton, Wisc.: American Girl Publishing, 2004.

Miller, Michael. *Absolute Beginner's Guide to Computer Basics.* 5th ed. Indianapolis: Que Publishing, 2009.

Nitta, Hideo, and Keita Takatsu. *The Manga Guide to Physics.* San Francisco: No Starch Press, 2009.

Peterson's. *Peterson's Summer Opportunities for Kids & Teenagers.* 26th ed. Lawrenceville, N.J.: Peterson's, 2008.

Salvadori, Mario. *The Art of Construction: Projects and Principles for Beginning Engineers and Architects.* 3d ed. Chicago: Chicago Review Press, 2000.

Sterrett, Andrew, ed. *101 Careers in Mathematics.* 2d ed. Washington, D.C.: Mathematical Association of America, 2003.

Takahashi, Shin. *The Manga Guide to Statistics.* San Francisco: No Starch Press, 2008.

VanCleave, Janice. *Janice VanCleave's Engineering for Every Kid: Easy Activities that Make Learning Science Fun.* Hoboken, N.J.: Wiley, 2007.

Vorderman, Carol. *How Math Works.* New York: Reader's Digest, 1999.

Walker, Jearl. *Flying Circus of Physics.* 2d ed. Hoboken, N.J.: Wiley, 2006.

White, Ron, and Timothy Edward Downs. *How Computers Work.* 9th ed. Indianapolis: Que Publishing, 2007.

Woods, Michael, and Mary B. Woods. *Ancient Machines: From Wedges to Waterwheels.* Minneapolis: Runestone Press, 1999.

Periodicals

Astronomy

http://www.astronomy.com

eGFI: Dream Up the Future
http://www.egfi-k12.org/read-the-magazine

PhysicsQuest
http://www.physicscentral.com/physicsquest

Plus Magazine
http://plus.maths.org

The Pre-Engineering Times
http://www.jets.org/publications/petimes.cfm

Time for Kids
http://www.timeforkids.com/TFK

Web Sites

A+ Math
http://www.aplusmath.com

AAA Math
http://www.aaamath.com

Accounting for Kids
http://www.accountingforkids.com

American Library Association: Great Web Sites for Kids
http://www.ala.org/greatsites

ARCHcareers.org
http://www.archcareers.org

Ask Dr. Math
http://mathforum.org/dr.math/dr-math.html

Ask the Space Scientist
http://image.gsfc.nasa.gov/poetry/ask/askmag.html

Astronomy Today
http://www.astronomytoday.com

Be a Math Teacher
http://www.nctm.org/resources/content.aspx?id=530

Be an Actuary
http://www.beanactuary.org

Careers in Optics
http://spie.org/x30120.xml

Computer History Museum
http://www.computerhistory.org

Computing Degrees and Careers
http://computingcareers.acm.org

CoolMath.com
http://coolmath.com

eGFI: Dream Up the Future
http://egfi-k12.org

Engineer Girl!
http://www.engineergirl.org

Exploring the Science of Light!
http://www.opticsforteens.org

Fermilab: Education
http://www.fnal.gov/pub/education/k-12_programs.html

Frank Potter's Science Gems: Mathematics
http://sciencegems.com/math.html

Free On-Line Dictionary of Computing
http://foldoc.org

Indexes of Biographies (Mathematicians)
http://www-groups.dcs.st-and.ac.uk/~history/BiogIndex.html

Intro to Astronomy
http://www.astronomy.com/asy/default.aspx?c=ps&id=6

Invention Dimension
http://web.mit.edu/invent/invent-main.html

Investing for Kids
http://library.thinkquest.org/3096

Kids & Money
http://www.ext.nodak.edu/extnews/pipeline/d-parent.htm

Kids' Finance
http://www.kidsfinance.com

Light in Action: Lasers, Cameras & Other Cool Stuff
http://spie.org/x30120.xml

Math Cats
http://www.mathcats.com

Math Is Fun
http://www.mathsisfun.com

Math Playground
http://www.MathPlayground.com

Math Words
http://www.mathwords.com/a_to_z.htm

Measurements Converter
http://www.convert-me.com/en

MinyanLand
http://www.minyanland.com

National Aeronautics and Space Administration: For Students: Grades K–4
http://www.nasa.gov/audience/forstudents/k-4

National Aeronautics and Space Administration: For Students: Grades 5–8
http://www.nasa.gov/audience/forstudents/5-8

National Inventors Hall of Fame
http://www.invent.org/hall_of_fame/1_0_0_hall_of_fame.asp

A New Universe to Discover: Careers in Astronomy
http://aas.org/education/careers.php

Operations Research: The Science of Better
http://www.scienceofbetter.org

Optics: Light at Work
http://spie.org/x30120.xml

PhysicsCentral
http://www.physicscentral.com

Physics Students
http://www.aps.org/careers/student

A Sightseer's Guide to Engineering
http://www.engineeringsights.org

Sloan Career Cornerstone Center
http://careercornerstone.org

Society of Exploration Geophysicists Kids
http://students.seg.org/kids

Space Weather.com
http://www.spaceweather.com

Start Here, Go Places
http://www.startheregoplaces.com

The Tech Museum of Innovation
http://www.thetech.org

Thinking of a Career in Applied Mathematics?
http://www.siam.org/careers/thinking.php

U.S. Department of Energy: For Students and Kids
http://www.energy.gov/forstudentsandkids.htm

U.S. Mint H.I.P. Pocket Change
http://www.usmint.gov/kids

Why Choose Computer Science & Engineering?
http://www.cs.washington.edu/WhyCSE

Index